In

Shadows

The Hope for a Better Future

Randy Moore

Copyright © 2025 Randy Moore

All rights are reserved.

Any unauthorized reproduction or use of this material is strictly forbidden. No part of this book may be reproduced or transmitted in any form or by any means—whether electronic or mechanical—such as photocopying, recording, or through any information storage and retrieval system without explicit written consent from the author.

We have made every reasonable effort to ensure the accuracy of the information presented in this publication. However, the author accepts no responsibility for any errors or omissions that may occur.

ISBN (Paperback): 9781964467955

ISBN (Hardcover): 9781964467962

Dedication

To my beloved wife, Natasha Moore, and our wonderful children, Randy Moore II and Kaylee Moore.

This book is dedicated to you, my guiding light and unwavering support. As Dr. Tony Wade beautifully expresses in his song "Journey", "I am grateful for my journey and that I'm standing here today", life is a series of steps taken together, and I am grateful for every step we share.

Proverbs reminds us, *"A man that findeth a wife findeth a good thing and obtaineth favor from the Lord."* You are my good thing, Natasha, the treasure I cherish every day. Thank you for your love, strength, and encouragement, which inspire me to reach for my dreams.

Randy and Kaylee, you are the joy of my heart and the motivation behind my words. I also look forward to the day when I can hold my future grandchildren in my arms. It is for you and them that I have chosen to break the curses and chains that have held our family back. I pray for a future filled with blessings, opportunity, and love, paving the way for generations to come.

May your journeys be filled with love, wisdom, and the same unwavering support that you have shown me.

Acknowledgement

As I reflect on the journey that led to the creation of this book, I am filled with gratitude for the many individuals who have played a pivotal role in shaping my narrative. This work is not solely my own; it is a tapestry woven from the threads of countless lives, experiences, and moments of support.

First and foremost, I want to express my deepest gratitude to God the Creator and my Savior Jesus Christ for guiding me through the highs and lows of my life. Your unwavering presence has been a source of strength and comfort, illuminating my path even in the darkest of times. I recognize that every moment of clarity and inspiration comes from a higher power, and I am eternally thankful for your grace and mercy.

I would like to extend my heartfelt appreciation to my wife, Natasha Moore. Your encouragement and unwavering belief in my ability to share my story have been invaluable to me. You have stood by my side through every challenge, providing the love and support that have fueled my determination. Thank you for being my rock and my inspiration; your faith in me has made all the difference.

To my children, Randy Moore II and Kaylee Moore, I want to acknowledge the immense joy and motivation you bring into my life. Your support and understanding have been a constant reminder of what truly matters. I hope that as you read these words, you see the love I have for you both and understand the lessons I wish to pass on. You inspire me to strive for a better future, not only for myself but for our family.

I want to extend my heartfelt appreciation to my oldest brother, whose request for a letter sparked the impetus for this reflection. Your encouragement and belief in the importance of sharing our story have been invaluable. This book is a testament to the bond we share and the love that underpins our relationship.

I would also like to express my gratitude to my other siblings—Kasey, Brandon, and Leisa—who have been both my companions and my motivation throughout this journey. Each of you has contributed to my story in unique ways, and I cherish the memories we have shared.

I am profoundly grateful to my grandmother, Faye Evelyn Moore, whose unwavering strength and guidance provided the foundation for my resilience. Your lessons, though often delivered with tough love, have shaped the person I am today. Thank you for instilling in me the values of perseverance and self-defense.

To my mother, Mable "Doris" Moore, I acknowledge the complexity of our relationship. Your struggles and triumphs have profoundly influenced my understanding of love and addiction. I hope this narrative honors the complicated nature of our bond and the lessons learned along the way.

I would also like to express my heartfelt gratitude to Sharon and Jeffery Miles, along with the entire Miles family. You took me in as a teenager, offering me a sense of belonging and treating me as one of your own. Your kindness and acceptance during a pivotal time in my life provided me with stability and love that I will always cherish. Thank you for embracing me and making me feel like family.

I would like to express my heartfelt gratitude to Alice Herron, lovingly known as Granny. Though she has since passed away, her stories and memories about my grandmother have been invaluable to me throughout this writing journey. Alice, who was my grandmother's sister in spirit rather than by blood, shared with me countless tales that enriched my understanding of family history. Her mother took my grandmother in after the untimely passing of her own mother, creating a bond that transcended bloodlines. I am forever grateful for the warmth and wisdom she imparted, which live on in these pages.

To the rest of the Herron family, who welcomed my grandmother into their home, I will always respect and appreciate your kindness. You treated us like family and showed nothing but love, and I will forever cherish the memory of my Granny, Alice Herron.

I would also like to extend my appreciation to Ms. Brookins, my fifth-grade teacher, whose sternness and unwavering belief in the power of prayer introduced me to a lifestyle that would become my own— Christianity. I am also thankful to Ms. Kirkendall, my high school English teacher, whose encouragement and belief in my potential inspired me to succeed in college, and to Mrs. Norris, my geometry teacher, whose support further motivated me to pursue higher education.

I owe a great debt of gratitude to Command Sergeant Major Richard Bell, who poured into my life during a time when I needed it the most. Additionally, I wish to acknowledge Candy Luster, my big sister, who cared for me during the times when my siblings were incarcerated and when Sharon and Jeff were on the road; your kindness will always be remembered.

I am grateful for Bishop and Evangelist Kiel, whose spiritual guidance has been invaluable, and to my non-blood brothers, Dr. Tony Wade and Apostle Jerome Williams, for accepting me as I am and for leading me spiritually in ways they may not fully realize.

I would like to extend my appreciation to Dr. Ernest Plata from Wiley College for his mentorship and even monetary support during a time of need. I also thank Dr. Don G. Hill, my mentor and big brother, who at times acted more like a father. He was the first person I met when I attended Wiley College, and I am grateful that we are still friends to this day.

My sincere thanks extend to Army National Guard Captains White and Wildrix, my company commanders at the 49th Armory Division 1/112 HHC, for their leadership. I also appreciate the support and encouragement from Lieutenant Colonel (Ret.) Geoffrey Powell and Dr. Michael Ampeles as I pursued my career in the medical field, along with Lieutenant

Colonel Scott Davis for his mentorship during my early years as an officer.

To my aunt Cat, Carolyn Norwood, thank you for always being there for me in both good times and bad. I am grateful for my sisters and brothers in Christ at Full Gospel Holy Temple, especially Lynn Charles Smith.

I cannot forget the entire Jenkins family, my sisters by heart—Tomika, Tamera, Tam, Tekel, my baby sister Trina, Nikki, and Dana; Aunts Wilma, Net-Net, and Denise; my mother-in-love La Ru Jenkins, and my father-in-love, Clifford Jenkins. To my goddaughters, Abby Neal, Ryan Grace, Giovanni Weber, and Reign Nathaniel you have all inspired me in countless ways.

I thank God for each and every one of you for your support, love, encouragement, and understanding. You have all played a vital role in shaping my life and making me who I am today.

I would like to acknowledge anyone I may have inadvertently missed—friends, teachers, counselors, and extended family members—who offered valuable insights and perspectives that helped shape my understanding of myself and the world around me.; your impact on my life has not gone unnoticed. I thank God for all of you for your support, love, encouragement, and understanding. You have all played a vital role in shaping my life and making me who I am today. Your words and actions have left a permanent mark on my life.

Finally, I want to acknowledge the readers of this book. Your willingness to engage with my story is a profound gift. I hope that within these pages, you find not only my reflections but also a sense of connection, understanding, and hope. Together, we can continue to learn from our past and strive for a brighter future.

Thank you all for being part of this journey. Your contributions have made this book possible, and for that, I am eternally grateful. Together, these individuals have contributed to this journey in profound ways, and I am grateful for each of you.

Thank you for being part of my life and for encouraging me to share my story.

Table of Contents

Introduction xviii

Chapter One The Journey Called Life 1

Chapter Two Fort Worth, Texas. 1950. 25

Chapter Three Bonds Without Blood 59

Chapter Four The Blue Bicycle 86

Chapter Five The Last Goodbye 104

Chapter Six 1305 Stewart to 2717 Ashcresent 122

Chapter Seven Choices and Consequences.............. 142

Chapter Eight The First Gun Shot............................. 158

Chapter Nine A False Role Model 173

Chapter Ten The Meadows and the Bloods............. 194

Chapter Eleven A Big Fight.. 212

Chapter Twelve September 1994 230

Chapter Thirteen Glen Garden's History 239

Chapter Fourteen The Projects................................... 254

Chapter Fifteen The Price of Loyalty 271

Chapter Sixteen When the Walls Close In 285

Letter From Me to You! 302

About The Author

Dr. Randy Moore hails from Fort Worth, Texas, where he has experienced a life filled with both challenges and wonderful moments. Growing up, Randy faced many obstacles that shaped who he is today. He lived in neighborhoods that were not always safe and witnessed events that were difficult to understand. Despite these hardships, he always held onto hope and faith, believing that God was guiding him through every tough situation.

One of Randy's earliest and most cherished memories is waking up one special morning to find a bright blue bicycle with a banana seat waiting for him. This moment felt like the beginning of his journey, filling him with excitement and joy. Although his childhood was filled with difficulties, Randy learned the importance of resilience and perseverance. He knew deep down that his faith in God would help him overcome any challenges he faced.

Randy dedicated himself to his education, working very hard in school. He graduated from Wiley University in Marshall, Texas, earning a Bachelor's degree in Biology. His love for learning led him to the UNT Health Science Center in Fort Worth, where he earned a Master's Degree. Never one to settle, he continued his studies and achieved his dream of obtaining a Doctor of Health Science Degree from Nova Southeastern University in Fort Lauderdale, Florida. Throughout his academic journey, Dr. Moore always gave glory to God, recognizing that his achievements were made possible through divine support.

In addition to his accomplishments in education, Dr. Moore serves his country as an Officer in the Texas Army National Guard. With over 27 years of dedicated service, he has deployed to Iraq, Afghanistan, and Guatemala. Today, he practices medicine as a Physician Associate in Family Medicine in Longview,

Texas, where he makes a difference in the lives of his patients.

Randy's personal life is equally fulfilling. He is happily married to his loving wife, Natasha, and they are the proud parents of two wonderful children, Randy II and Kaylee Ann. Together, they create a warm and loving family environment, always cherishing their moments together. They emphasize the importance of giving thanks to God for the blessings in their lives and strive to be a source of kindness and inspiration to others.

Dr. Randy Moore's journey teaches us that no matter how tough life can be, having faith in God and putting in hard work can help us achieve our dreams. His story encourages everyone to embrace their own experiences and to remember that with determination and support, they can make a positive impact in the world around them.

Page Left Blank Intentionally

Introduction

"The darkest hour has only sixty minutes"

I know you don't know me, but that feels irrelevant because I have a story to tell. A story that's been buried for too long. A story that needs to be heard—not just by me but by my brothers, too. They don't have a voice right now. They're silenced in one way or another, and it's time someone spoke for them. So that's what I'm here to do. I'm here to speak for the ones who can't.

I've spent so many years keeping quiet, keeping everything inside. But I can't anymore. The weight of it all is too much. The regrets, the mistakes, the broken pieces of our lives that no one ever talks about. It's all been sitting on my chest like a heavy rock, and I can't carry it alone anymore. I have to speak. I have to tell this story.

My brothers? They're not just names on a page. They're pieces of me, pieces of us—lost, hurting, broken. But they're not just their mistakes. They're not just the things they've done wrong. They're human, just like I am. And they deserve to be heard. That's why I'm writing this. To give them their voice back. To let the world see who they are. Not the versions they've been painted as. Not the prisoners, the outcasts, the failures. They are so much more than that.

And honestly? It hurts. To look back on the things we've been through. To realize the places we've ended up. Some days, I can't even recognize the faces of the men my brothers have become. It's like we're all strangers, lost in our pain. I wonder every day if I missed something. If there was a moment, I could've stepped in and saved them before everything fell apart. I ask myself—was I enough? Did I do enough?

But the truth is, I don't have answers. I'm just here to tell the truth, raw and unfiltered. This book isn't just my story. It's theirs. It's ours. It reflects a life we didn't ask for, but somehow, it's the one we got. This book is for my brothers.

So yeah, this book is about the past. But it's also about the future. What can we learn from all the broken pieces, all the hurt, and all the mistakes? Maybe through sharing this story, we can find some peace. Maybe the pain will start to heal. But even if it doesn't, I'll tell it anyway because it may help someone else.

But I can't be silent anymore. I can't let the world forget who we were, who we are. So I'll tell you everything. All the things we didn't say. All the things we didn't want anyone to know.

But first, I'll ask whether you're ready to hear the truth because it's not easy. It's not clean. But it's ours. And I promise you, by the end, you'll know us like we've always known each other.

Let's Begin

It's funny how life works out sometimes. I never thought I'd be sitting here—alone—writing about everything that's happened to me and my brothers. But here I am, with a cup of coffee long since gone cold, staring out the window, trying to figure out where to start. The past keeps creeping into my head, and the more I think about it, the harder it is to hold back.

So I guess this is it. This is me telling our story. My brother's story is the one I never thought I'd be the one to share. But someone has to tell it, right? And if I'm being honest, it's harder to keep it inside than to say it out loud.

Growing up, things seemed pretty straightforward. We were just kids, running around, thinking life was one big adventure. We spent days playing in the yard, getting into trouble, sneaking orange slices from Grama when she wasn't looking. It was the kind of childhood you'd expect—full of laughter and promise. But none of us realized then that the world wasn't as perfect as we thought.

I never imagined things would end up this way. Never imagined I'd be the only one left standing, with my brothers in places I can't reach. You could say I never expected to be the one left to tell the story, but here I am with all these memories that weigh me down. And I need to get them out.

It's not easy to look back, to face the things that happened, the things we did, the things we lost. Some of it still hurts too much to even think about. But writing it down feels like the only way to make sense of all the chaos. This is my way of finally saying what needs to be said, not just for me, but for all of us—my brothers, my family.

So here I sit, coffee forgotten, trying to put the words on paper. I don't know if I'll ever have all the answers, but I know this: we were more than the mess we became. We were more than the mistakes. And maybe, just maybe, putting it all down will make some sense of it all.

And if you're reading this, you may see what I mean.

The decision to write this book wasn't something I took lightly. Honestly, it's been eating at me for a long time. There's so much left unsaid, so many pieces of our lives that no one knows about. My brothers don't get to tell their side of the story. They can't. They're either too far gone or locked away where no one can hear them. So I guess it's up to me now. I need to speak for them. I need to give them a voice where they've been silent for so long.

I'm Randy, the third oldest of four brothers. I'm the one who's still standing—still here, trying to make sense of everything.

Let me introduce you to my brothers.

First, there's Kevin, the oldest. Kevin is the strong, reliable one. He is serious-minded and mature for his age, often putting others' needs ahead of his own. He is the responsible "oldest child" figure, looking after our mother and developing a sense of self-reliance.

Kevin was the kind of guy who didn't just talk about what he wanted to do; he did it. And he did it with passion. But somewhere along the way, things went sideways for him. That fire inside him burned too hot and ended up burning him. He made decisions that led him down a path none of us could follow. But back when we were kids, I'd never have imagined that for him. He was the guy who seemed to have it all figured out.

Next is Kasey, the second oldest. Though quiet and introverted, Kasey possesses inner resilience and can express himself through creativity and thoughtfulness. His timidity hides a deep sensitivity, often seeking connection in ways that others don't notice. That's why he kept so much to himself and pushed people away. Kasey's strength was his ability to hold it together, but it came at a price. Eventually, that price was too much.

Then there's me, the third oldest, Randy. I've always been caught between Kevin's fiery determination and Kasey's quiet introspection. I've always felt like I had to keep the balance, to hold the pieces together when the cracks started to show. I'm the one telling this story but also the one who's been left behind. I can't explain it, but I've always felt like I had a responsibility—maybe to fix things or keep going when it seemed like everyone else was falling apart. But that's where I am now. The last one standing.

Finally, there's Brandon, the youngest boy. Brandon's fierce need to protect others stems from his raging childhood, and his strength lies in his ability to survive and make others notice him, even if it means using violence. Deep down, he craves love and validation, but his anger often masks his vulnerability.

Each of us had our own roles, struggles, and strengths. We were different, no doubt about it. But no matter what, we were family.

Growing up, we didn't have much. We lived in a neighborhood where survival meant more than anything else—where getting by was a daily battle. The streets were rough, and the world didn't give us a break. But we made it work. We had to. There wasn't any other option. We learned early on that no one else would if you didn't look out for yourself. And if you didn't stick together, the world would tear you apart.

We fought for the minor things—like socks and underwear or who drank the last of the milk or ate the last piece of chicken, and a few minutes of peace. We fought with each other, fought against the world, and fought for our spot in it. And there were moments when we fought with each other so hard it felt like the whole house was coming down. Family arguments, things said in anger that we never took back. There were a lot of those. We were all different and had different ways of dealing with things, and sometimes that caused friction. Sometimes, it felt like the only way to survive was to keep pushing forward, even if it meant stepping on someone.

But even with all the fighting, some moments made it all worth it. Times when we came together—when one of us needed help, and the others showed up without question. Those moments, though few and far between, are the ones that stuck with me. They shaped us. They shaped me. I learned early on that no matter how much we bickered, we were still brothers. No matter how much we hurt each other, that bond was always there.

Looking back, it's clear that we were shaped by those moments—by the fights, the struggles, the tiny wins we had. And somehow, even with all the chaos, we stayed close enough to one another to keep going. But not without scars. Not without pain. And not without those moments that would later define the men we became.

But that's just the beginning. You'll see what I mean as we go. Every chapter will dig deeper into my brothers' struggles and what led us down these problematic paths. The choices, the moments that changed everything. And I'm not going to sugarcoat it. I can't because there's no easy way to tell this. There's no simple explanation for what happened, and I don't have all the answers. But I need to tell you anyway. Remember, it's a one-chapter or one story about 4 lives.

It's the kind of thing that makes you question everything. Where did we go wrong? What did we miss? How did we let this happen? I'm going to tell you, but you'll have to wait. That story is more significant than you think, and it's not one I can rush through.

But trust me, when you get to it, you'll see. You'll understand why this whole thing—this book, this story—matters. Because the truth is, none of us were ever who we seemed. We all had our secrets! So, stick with me. There's so much more to come.

Chapter One

The Journey Called Life

Love is the thread that weaves strength into the fabric of a family, even when life tries to tear it apart.

Our lives were never like this, as they are now. It's hard to believe how far we've fallen. Some days, I barely recognize the faces of my brothers in the headlines, their names stained by things they never imagined they'd do. It wasn't supposed to be this way.

That's the thing about life – it's funny like that. You don't see the cracks forming until you've stepped into the crater. As a kid, none of us could have guessed that we'd end up like this, scattered across the world in pieces, and me… I'm the only one left out here trying to make sense of it all.

Growing up, our days were filled with the laughter you hear in movies. Simple, right? Playing football in the street with no shoes on, sneaking orange slices or strawberries from the icebox when Grama wasn't looking, and the smell of fresh-cut grass mixing with the sunburnt air were the moments that made us feel like we could take on anything. We were the Moore brothers—nothing could touch us, or so we thought.

But there's something about those perfect moments when you're a child, something we don't realize until it's too late: Not every kid has them. Not every home feels safe, and not every family is whole, no matter how hard we wish it were. And somewhere between those moments of happiness, something changed. I don't know when exactly. Maybe it was gradual. Maybe it happened all at once. But somehow, we were no longer just four brothers running around without a care. Now, I'm the only one left to tell the story.

I lean back in my chair, the photo album resting gently in my lap, my eyes drawn to one image. It's a picture of Grama Faye Evelyn Moore, my mother's mother, sitting on the porch of our old house. She's in a wheelchair, though she only used it for sitting, her legs crossed and her fingers lightly intertwined across her lap. She's wearing a sleeveless polyester dress, her smile more of a smirk, and her glasses perched on her nose. The background captures the green of our house, with the address 1327 visible, and as I turned the page to the next, I saw another beautiful photo where Grama Faye had just finished talking to the insurance man, who's parked in his gold two-seat Pontiac Fiero—something my family would know exactly, that specific moment. Kevin's beside her on his bike, his grin wide and genuine, in one of those rare instances when he wasn't lost in his own world. They both look so peaceful, untouched by the chaos that would come later.

I stare at that photo, something heavy tugging at my chest for a while. This picture doesn't just show the two of them, but it feels like it's pulling me backward, like a gateway to a time when things were more transparent and straightforward. The sounds of my childhood flood back in a wave—the creak of the metal chain-link fence in the yard, the slam of the screen door, and the steady hum of a fan blowing at night through an open window. They all come rushing back, familiar and comforting, like the soundtrack of those simpler days. I remember how Grama always made everything feel safe. Everything would be okay when we were with her, no matter what happened outside those old wooden doors.

Family gatherings at her house felt more like a small party. The grown-ups would sit out on the porch, and the sounds of 1970s and 1980s R&B or blues— Luther Vandross, Marvin Gaye, Earth, Wind & Fire, and Prince—would play in the background. Coors beer in hand, they'd swap old stories, laughing and fussing, while all the kids ran around, playing hide-and-go-seek. Grama always yelled and fussed about something, but we were used to it by then. Even though she'd yell and curse, something about being near her made everything feel better, like no matter how tough things got, they'd get better just by being around her. Then there were the quieter moments, just the two of us sitting on the front porch, sunlight stretching long across the yard. She'd tell stories, sometimes ones I'd heard a thousand times before, but I'd always listen like it was the first.

I look at the picture again. She's beautiful, you know? In her younger days, she was slim, but by the time I knew her, she had a more round shape, with skinny legs and a wider abdominal area. Her smile would always bring out a dimple on the right side of her cheek, and that dimple, along with the mole near her lip, was the little detail that made her so distinctly hers; it was like her trademark. You couldn't help but smile with her, even if you were feeling down. And it wasn't just that. There was an elegance in the way she carried herself. The way she moved, the way she held her head high, and her posture were always straight but never rigid. There was something about her presence that made you feel like you were in the presence of someone… important. Not in the way that someone wealthy or powerful might make you feel, but in a quiet, subtle way. She had seen so much, understood so much, and still chose to embrace life with grace.

I can't explain it, but she left a permanent mark on me. Every time I close my eyes, I can see her face. And I can still hear her voice, powerful, just like she always was. I don't know if we realized how much she shaped us back then, but I sure do now. Even in the darkest times, I can almost hear her telling me, telling all of us, that there's still hope. No matter how bad things get, you don't give up on family.

But there were things that even she didn't speak of. I don't know if it was because she didn't want to burden us with them or because she believed it was better left in the past. But every time I think about her, I can't help but wonder what we never knew. Her life wasn't just about love and warmth. There was a history there, one she carried like a shadow, and it was always there, lurking in the corners of the house. You could almost feel it when she'd pause for a moment too long when telling a story, like she was carefully picking her words, deciding what part of the past to leave out.

Sometimes, I wish I could ask her more—about her youth and life before she became the matriarch of our family. I've heard bits and pieces, half-formed stories told by my uncles, but it's like there was an unspoken rule that we never pried too deep. She had a way of turning every conversation back to the present, always steering it away from anything that could cause discomfort. But I wonder, even now, if I could have cracked open that shell she built so carefully around herself. What would I have found?

I think about my mother now. She's gone, too, and I wonder if she felt the same way. My mom, Mable Doris---, preferred to be called Doris, a quiet strength in her own right, but she was different from Grama. There was something in her eyes that carried the same burden of history, something I could never quite put my finger on. My mother had a way of holding things in, never showing when she was hurt. I wonder if that's what she learned from Grama —how to hide the wounds so well that even your closest family would never know they were there.

I look back at the photo again. My grandmother's face is so serene in this picture. But I know better than to believe it was always that way. I know that behind her soft smile, strength came from surviving things we can't even begin to imagine. And that's the thing about people like her—they don't wear their wounds on the outside. They hide them, protect them. Only when you stop and look you see how much they've carried.

As I flip through the photo album pages, I realize how much of her I've taken with me, even if I never asked her about the past. Her resilience, her grace under pressure, and most of all, her love. She ensured we never went without, even when nothing was left. But sometimes, it wasn't enough. Sometimes, the cracks couldn't be mended, no matter how hard she tried to hold it all together. And now, with my brothers scattered, imprisoned, or lost to their demons, I can't help but think that maybe, in the end, the thing we all needed most was something more than just love.

I now think about the empty spaces—the things left unsaid, the memories never fully shared. Grama's voice again tells me, "Don't give up on family, Randy. No matter how bad it gets." But I can't help but wonder if she ever saw this coming. It would eventually crumble if she knew the very thing she spent her life protecting. She always believed in us and the good we could do, but in the end, I'm left here alone, holding the fragments of a family that no longer exists as we knew it.

I trace my finger over the photo's edges, the image is faded and distant, almost far-off. In this picture, Grama looks untouched by the world's troubles—her face serene, her posture elegant. But when I think about it, I know the woman in that photo wasn't the full story. Life changes people, and it changed all of us, even her. The woman in the picture might have been gentle and warm-hearted, but the truth is, Grama was never just soft-spoken. She had the fire inside her—a strength you couldn't ignore. Her quiet elegance was only a small part of who she was.

Grama was a force of nature when it came to her family. She didn't back down, no matter what life threw her way. You didn't mess with Faye Evelyn Moore. She stood her unflinching ground and held us together with a resilience we didn't fully understand then.

There was something in how she carried herself—how her hands gripped the arms of a chair, and she would grit her teeth when she fussed or when something wasn't right. She ensured her family was always taken care of, and when things got tough, we saw that quiet strength that could move mountains when needed.

Most people didn't know the depths of what Grama had endured. Losing her mother as a child had shaped her in ways we could never fully understand. She grew up fast, shouldering burdens no child should bear, but she made sure we, her children and grandchildren, never felt that weight. She shielded us from storms, even if it meant weathering them herself. And, believe me, life didn't let up. There was no shortage of struggle, but you'd never hear her complain. She never did. Instead, she worked harder, loved harder, and kept the family intact.

That love, combined with her strength, kept our family intact. When we messed up, she picked up the pieces. Always, without hesitation. But as much as she gave, she didn't make it look easy. She couldn't—because it wasn't. And that's what I see now. As I flip through these pages, remembering her, I realize that her love wasn't about giving us everything we wanted. It was about giving us what we needed. The lessons she passed down and the strength she built into us are the things I carry with me.

Grama was like the glue that held our family together. Without her, we wouldn't have made it through the tough times. She always made sure we had food to eat and a place to stay. Even when we didn't have water, electricity, or gas, she kept us safe and warm. Simple meals like beans with ground meat and rice with butter and sugar were the staples, and no matter what, Grama always made sure we had enough to fill our bellies.

She was also the person responsible for the family. Grama never did drugs, but she enjoyed her alcohol—a little brandy or cold Coors beer now and then. She'd learned to appreciate a drink from her club days when she was younger. Grama had been petite and pretty in her youth, with a dimple on her right cheek and a bright smile. But by the time I knew her, she had a different look. She had developed central obesity, with skinny legs but a wider abdominal area, a condition that was a product of the health problems she faced, including diabetes. She wore wide-brimmed glasses that became part of her signature style, along with that same dimple and a mole just above her upper lip.

Grama always walked purposefully, as though she had somewhere important to be. Her eyes constantly scanned the surroundings, almost as if she were checking if anyone was up to no good. She didn't trust people easily and often expected the worst from them. Unlike the gentle, soft-spoken image of grandmothers, Grama was loud and direct. She rarely smiled and could swear like a sailor, but we knew beneath all that gruffness, she loved us—she just didn't say it like most people did. Even though she yelled and cursed, she never needed to say, "I love you." Her actions spoke louder than words ever could.

Grama was thoughtful in her own way. Her friends would come to her for help reading or signing their names because many couldn't read or write. She was good with money, always making the most of what she had. She might not have said things like, "We're going to make it," but she showed her love in the unique ways she spoke to us and how she cared for us. She had a way of teasing that could be tough but also funny, like calling me an illegitimate child, and she would use the curse word that referred to an illegitimate child. It was just one of her ways of shaping our understanding of life, challenging us and sometimes making us laugh even when it was rough.

Her language was full of these colorful, sharp sayings. If I ever said, "But I thought," she'd respond with, "Don't nobody thought but old folks and fools, and you don't look like an old folk to me. "If I would say something like, "I'm thirsty", she might joke and say something like, "Well, I'm Friday. Let's get together on Saturday and make a Sunday." She had a knack for humor, and even when we complained about not having somewhere to sit, she'd tell us, "Sit on your fist and lean back on your thumb."

Her humor, always sharp and quick, was unforgettable. She'd joke with us, saying things like "See you later, alligator," followed by "After a while, crocodile." But sometimes, Grama would slip, and a stronger word would come out—no sugarcoating in her world. And when we did something foolish, she'd shake her head and say, "You don't know your butt from a hole in the ground," though she used a different word for "butt" that made us laugh, even when we knew she was serious. It was her way of showing disapproval while still keeping things light-hearted.

Mornings felt special because I'd often wake up to the smell of her making instant coffee—Sanka, of course. After all, it was caffeine-free. The smell of it brought back so many memories. I'd find her at the table, carefully picking through beans, pulling out the bits of dirt. That smell, like rain hitting the ground, always felt nostalgic, and sometimes she'd even share the bits of dirt with me, joking that it was a treat.

In the kitchen, Grama was always cooking. I remember how she fried chicken, ensuring her meat was soaking in the sink before cooking it. The scent of bleach would always be in the air when she cleaned, a part of her daily routine that made our home feel safe and familiar.

While Grama didn't tuck us in at night, she always ensured we had a place to sleep—a bed, a couch, or even a makeshift pallet on the floor. She never said, "I love you," but when she wanted to show affection, she'd offer us a treat, like an orange slice, and that was her way of saying it. If something happened that hurt our feelings, Grama wouldn't apologize in the usual way. Instead, she'd hand us a piece of gum, and we understood it was her way of apologizing.

You'd often find Grama sitting on the porch with a cigarette and a drink, chatting with her friends while we ran around outside. She'd laugh and tell stories, and sometimes when she drank too much, we'd take care of her the next morning when she was sick. Those were the only times we ever saw her cry—when she was drunk. But despite her tough exterior, Grama was our rock, always holding us together, even when life wasn't easy.

Through all the yelling, the cursing, and the tough love, Grama's legacy was clear. She may not have said "I love you" the way we expected, but she showed it in everything she did. She gave us what we needed—strength, discipline, and a deep sense of family.

I turn the page of the album, the sound of the paper folding under my fingertips almost as heavy as the weight of the memories it holds. The next photo is of my mother. Now, let me tell you about my mother, Mable Doris Moore, though she preferred to be called Doris. Momma was a beautiful woman—light-skinned, around five foot six, with smooth skin and light brown eyes. She had a soft, gentle voice that could calm you down even when everything around us seemed chaotic. But she wasn't one to be pushed around. She had an inner fire, a fierce protectiveness that could surface when it was needed. She loved having fun with us, often playing pretend games like doctor or office, creating worlds full of imagination and laughter.

Momma In 1978

However, life wasn't always easy for momma. She struggled with addiction, specifically crack cocaine, for as long as I could remember. As a child, I didn't fully understand its weight, but as I grew older, the toll it took on her life became undeniable. I remember how she'd close the curtains and cover the windows with blankets, convinced that people were watching her, even when it was just the TV. Sometimes, she acted strangely, like the police were spying on her through the television screen.

Momma had a lot of fears that came with the addiction. She often thought the police were watching her, even when the TV turned off, showing that little white line in the middle of the screen—she was sure it was a hidden camera. At night, we'd have to turn off all the lights and huddle together in one room because she thought someone was outside watching us.

There were dark moments when she resorted to risky things to support her addiction. Sometimes, she would disappear for weeks, only to return, apologetic and full of guilt. But it was a cycle—one that was hard to break. She would walk the streets, trying to find money however she could, sometimes even selling things from our house. I didn't understand it all as a child, but I knew it hurt her and us.

Money was always a problem for momma. She wasn't good at managing it, and more often than not, we had to help take care of her as we grew older. She had dropped out of school in the eleventh grade, and I often wondered if the drugs affected her ability to think clearly. Grama used to say that momma wasn't "quite wrapped too tight," and sometimes I agreed with her. Despite that, momma did have moments when she was trying to pull herself together. There were brief stretches where she found a job and even managed to open a bank account. But those times never lasted long. She would relapse, lose her job, and find herself back in the same cycle.

One of my clearest memories is when momma wrote checks at stores like Kmart to buy things we needed, even though she didn't have the money to cover them. She'd use the checks to get cash, which she'd spend on drugs. This caused a lot of trouble, and I remember hearing about her arrest warrant because of the bad checks. Momma was always afraid of the police, especially after an encounter when a police officer asked if she was Mable Moore, and she had to admit it. From then on, she went by Doris Escobar, especially when she was trying to hide from the law.

As momma got older, her body began showing signs of everything she had been through. She walked with a limp, her once-strong spirit had softened, and she became quieter. But she never lost that fiery edge when it mattered. After Grama passed, Momma struggled to keep everything together. She didn't have a steady place to live and sometimes stayed in a shelter or with various people. She would find temporary jobs, but the addiction always had its hold on her.

Eventually, she found stability, got a house, and convinced me to move in with her. But just like before, it didn't last long—drugs took hold of her again. She lived with my sister and her kids while relying on government assistance. It was eerily similar to how Grama had lived with her children when momma was young. Momma passed away at the age of 46. In her last years, she found peace with Christ, but by then, the damage to her body was too great. She died suffering from liver failure, a casualty of the many battles she'd fought throughout her life.

Even with all her struggles, momma left a mark on our family. She was a mother who loved fiercely, even though she fought demons we couldn't always understand. She was also a woman who carried the weight of so many secrets, things she never shared with anyone—things I wish I could've known. But despite everything, she was ours, and we loved her, even when it was hard to understand why things turned out the way they did.

And when I look at her photo now, I see a woman who tried, loved, and fought in her own way. Her story is full of twists and turns, and though I can't fully understand it all, I know one thing for sure: Doris, my mother, left us with lessons on love, resilience, and the complexity of life. Even when it all seemed lost, she showed me that strength can come from even the most broken places.

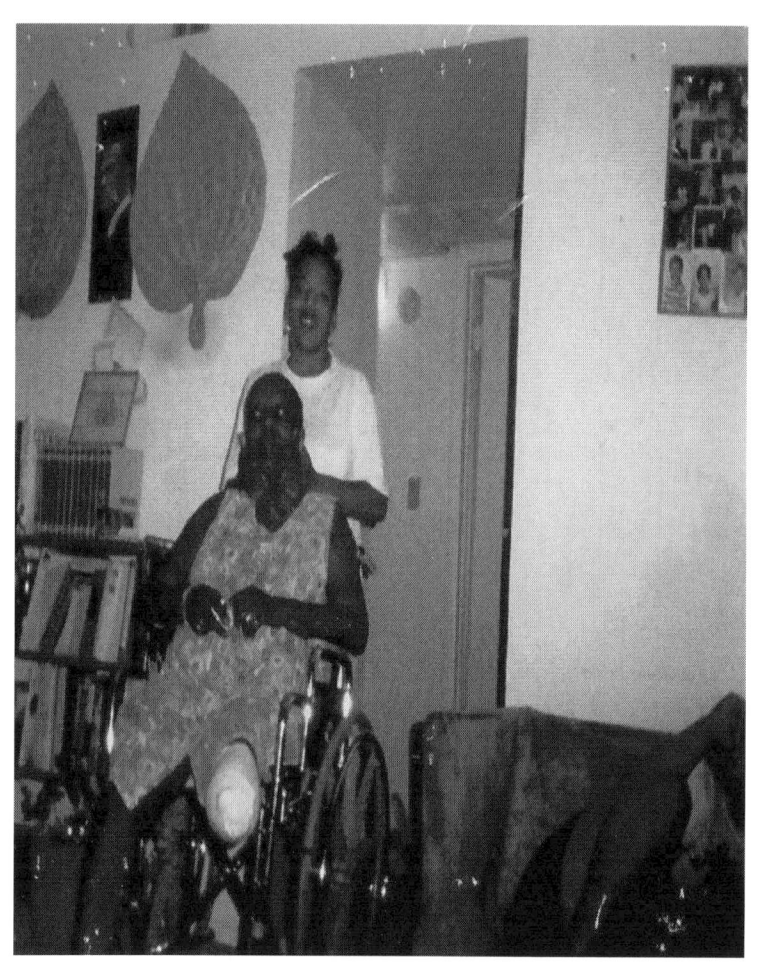

Momma And (Grama)

Chapter Two

Fort Worth, Texas. 1950.

Sometimes, the name you are given isn't the one you are meant to carry.

The house was quiet when I stepped inside, the kind of quiet that thickened the air. I could hear the soft, muffled sounds of my shoes sinking into the worn carpet as I walked through the hall. Sunlight streamed through the window, casting a warm glow that highlighted the stillness, making everything feel as if it were stuck in time. I wasn't sure why I had come today, but something had drawn me back here. It had been years since I last visited our old neighborhood, yet I knew she was the one person who might still remember the old stories—stories about Dickie, the boy no one spoke about much anymore.

I found her in the kitchen, just as I remembered, sitting at the kitchen table, smoking a cigarette. Her back was a little more hunched now, she was thinner, and her hair had turned silver, but she still wore that same warm smile.

"Well, look who's here," she said, her voice still firm but slightly softer than I remembered. "What brings you around this way, child?" "I was talking to my Uncle Dickie," I replied, leaning against the doorframe. "He found some old papers. From when he was born." At the mention of his name, Ms. Alice Herron—Granny, as we called her—paused.

Growing up, we always believed she was Grama's sister, only to discover later that they were not blood relatives. She didn't turn around, but her hands stopped moving, and for a moment, the kitchen felt even quieter than before. A slow sigh escaped her lips, the kind of sigh that suggested she was lost in thoughts of the past, memories I couldn't quite grasp. "Hmm. Dickie," she murmured, almost to herself.

"That boy... he brought much joy to our family, even if his situation added a bit of chaos to it all." She smiled softly as if the memories warmed her heart despite the challenges.

I stepped closer, my heart beating a little faster. "What do you remember about that time?" I asked. "About when Dickie was born?"

She turned to face me, her eyes narrowing just slightly like she was trying to figure out if I was ready for what she was about to say. "Well, it wasn't a happy time for Faye, unlike you might think. Not in the way people think of babies being born into the world with joy and celebration. No, it was different. There was something in the air. A feeling. A heaviness that I don't think anyone talked about, but we all knew."

I waited, trying to absorb what she was saying. "What do you mean?" I asked softly, not sure if I wanted to know the answer.

She turned and took another puff of her cigarette slowly. "You'll never really know, not unless you were there. But I'll tell you this—when Dickie was born, Faye's world changed. There was a decision made that day: something quiet, something heavy. It wasn't about joy or excitement. It was... something else. Something that no one ever really spoke about. Not out loud, anyway." And then she told me;

The air in the hospital room felt heavy, thick with something unspoken. It was crowded, but the room's stillness made it seem like time had slowed. It was as if the world outside was holding its breath, waiting for something to happen. No one could have known, but something was about to unfold that would change everything.

The room felt colder than it should have. The nurses exchanged quiet looks, sensing it but couldn't explain why. The baby, newly born, seemed different. His cries, though ordinary in sound, carried a strange weight, echoing deeper than anyone expected. It was as if this baby, this boy, was already bringing a warning that no one could understand.

Faye Evelyn Moore, known to everyone as Fats, lay exhausted in the hospital bed. Her body was drained, but her eyes told a different story—there was no joy, no celebration. She wasn't smiling down at her newborn child. Instead, her gaze was distant, troubled, as if something inside her knew that the road ahead would be anything but easy. She didn't look at him like a new mother would. There was a quiet sorrow in her eyes, a sense of conflict, a feeling that she was already bracing herself for what was to come.

When the nurse, gently and with care, asked, "What's the baby's name?" Faye didn't answer right away. She looked down at the child as though trying to figure out how to respond, as if she had no idea what to say. The silence in the room stretched on for a moment, and all the eyes seemed to wait for her to speak.

Finally, she answered, her voice steady but lacking warmth, "His name is just Dickie."

Just Dickie. No last name. No middle name. Just Dickie. The words were simple, but something about them felt heavy. No one in the room understood what it meant then, but it was a name that carried a sense of finality. It was as if she had decided, at that moment, that this child would be marked by something far different from what anyone might have expected.

The absence of a last name was strange and unsettling. It left a lingering question: why wasn't there more? But no one knew how much that missing piece would matter back then. No one realized that this boy—this child—would go on to have a life that defied the expectations of everyone around him.

Dickie's birth wasn't the start of something every day. From the beginning, his life would be tangled up in family secrets, chaos, and uncertainty. He wasn't the firstborn in the family, but he would be the one who marked the beginning of something different, something wild and unpredictable. Lawrence, his older brother, and Jean Ann, his little sister, were already part of a world full of confusion and difficulty, and Dickie would be dragged into it all, whether he was ready or not.

As Dickie grew, he would come to realize that his name—just Dickie—was more than just a label. It was a sign of something deeper that would shape his whole life. His story was only beginning, but already, the path ahead seemed unclear, as if the very air around him had been changed by the mysterious way he had entered the world.

Years later, as Dickie would look back on it all, he would understand that his name, that simple "Dickie," was more than anyone could have known. It was a name that would mark him for life, tying him to a family and a far-from-ordinary history.

Dickie's first memory stays with him like a shadow, never fully leaving. He remembers standing in the front yard, side by side with his older brother Lawrence and his younger sister Jean Ann. The three stood together, unsure of what was happening around them. It was a simple moment, but in hindsight, Dickie would realize that it marked the beginning of the confusion, the uncertainty, and the chaos that would follow them through their lives.

Jean Ann was just a little girl back then. She was smaller than the rest, her laughter always echoing. But then, one day, she was gone. Disappeared without a trace. It didn't make sense. Where did she go? What happened to her?

In the 1950s, things were different. Resources to help find missing children—predominantly African American children—didn't exist the way they do today. There was no Amber Alert, no community support, and no real way to discover what happened to someone missing. Jean Ann's disappearance was met with silence. No one asked questions. No one seemed to care enough to search. The authorities were too busy with their world to worry about the safety of a little black girl. So, Jean Ann's name slowly faded into the background, like so many others, forgotten by a world that wasn't built for people like her.

But that wasn't the end of the story.

Years later, Dickie would learn something that would change everything he thought he knew about his family. He would learn the truth about his father, Spike. For a long time, Dickie didn't even know who his father was. He grew up without the kind of father figure other kids had, and the mystery of who his father was lingered in his mind like a question with no answer.

Then, one day, Miss Pearl came to Faye's house. Miss Pearl was Spike's mother, but she had never known about his other child with Faye, she only knew about Jean Ann. She came to check on Jean Ann, worried about her well-being, but what she didn't know was that the child she thought was Spike's only daughter was also Dickie's sister.

When Miss Pearl found out, she was shocked. "You mean, that's Spike's kid too?" she asked, staring at Dickie like she had just learned something that didn't make sense. Faye nodded slowly, her tired eyes still heavy from years of struggle. She didn't know what to say. She had never told Miss Pearl about Dickie. She never told anyone. The secret had been kept for so long, even from Miss Pearl.

Miss Pearl's surprise turned into concern, but she didn't know the full story. She never knew that Spike had kept Dickie a secret, just like everything else about his life. She didn't know the truth about the affair between Spike and Faye. Spike had kept that part of his life hidden for so long. But the truth was undeniable now, and it complicated everything.

Spike's affair with Faye had been a secret buried too deep. And when Spike's wife found out, it didn't take long for the fighting to begin. Faye and Spike's wife were two women who would never get along. Their lives collided with anger and resentment, and Dickie saw it all. He could feel the tension, the bitterness that hung in the air whenever those two women came face to face. The arguments were loud, painful, and hard to ignore. But the most profound hurt came when Dickie realized the full extent of what had happened. He wasn't just a child caught in the middle—he was a living reminder of a secret that had torn families apart.

And then, the truth hit Dickie harder than anything ever had before: Spike, the man who was supposed to be his father, had other children, other families he had kept hidden from the world. Dickie wasn't the only one. There were others, brothers and sisters Dickie never knew. And as the pieces of his family's broken puzzle started to come together, the truth became clearer—Spike had never really been the father Dickie needed. He had never been the father to anyone.

It was painful for Dickie to accept. He had spent so many years wondering why his real father, Spike, wasn't there for him. But when he learned about the other kids, the other families Spike had built without him, something inside Dickie shifted. He wasn't the first choice. He wasn't even part of the original picture. He was just another secret.

But that secret would shape his life in ways he couldn't yet understand. It would tie him to a history he didn't want and force him to carry the weight of family secrets that no child should ever have to bear. The more Dickie learned, the more he realized how little he truly knew about the world he had been born into. And in the silence that followed, as everyone continued to pretend nothing was wrong, Dickie had to find his own way. He had to learn to navigate a world of half-truths, lies, and broken families.

As the years passed, Dickie would look back at those moments, at the absence of his father and the mystery surrounding his name. And he would know — from the very beginning, his life had been marked by something bigger than himself. Something that would continue to follow, shape, and define who he became.

The tension between Spike's family members grew as the years went by. Dickie, now older, started searching for the truth about his half-siblings, the children Spike had fathered with other women. He felt something deep inside, a pull to understand his family and discover who he was. It wasn't easy. He found bits and pieces, connections with other children Spike had left behind, and each discovery added weight to the growing mystery of his father's life.

The search wasn't just about knowing the truth it was about finding a place where Dickie could belong, a place where he could finally understand who he was in this tangled family web. But even as Dickie uncovered more, he began to see how divided the family really was, how every connection was filled with secrets and lies.

Things took a darker turn when Jean Ann, his little sister, was kidnapped by Spike's family. They took her from the Southside of Fort Worth, where they lived in poverty, to Stop Six—a more affluent area at that time, though still far from rich. Spike's family thought this move would give Jean Ann a better life and a chance to escape the rough edges of their world. However, for Jean Ann, the change was more than just moving to a different neighborhood. It marked the beginning of another chapter in her life, one where she would have to adapt to a new kind of family and a life far removed from what she had known.

In Stop Six, Jean Ann's world began to change. A new way of life surrounded her, and it wasn't long before she started to adjust. But even as things seemed to be looking up, Jean Ann had no idea that her life would face another upheaval that would pull her away from the life she had just begun to build.

Roy Lee, Granny's brother—and the person we always believed to be Grama's brother—spotted Jean Ann one day in Stop Six and hurried back to share the news with Grama. They had been looking for months, trying to track her down. When they finally found her, they didn't waste any time. This discovery set off a chain of events that would change everything for Jean Ann. She was taken from Stop Six and moved again—this time to California.

Jean Ann's life became a whirlwind between different families and worlds. She was always on the move, never able to settle down or find the peace she so desperately needed. Each new place, each new family, only added to the confusion, and she was left to navigate a life that felt like it was always in motion.

Meanwhile, back in Fort Worth, Miss Pearl felt a deep guilt for not knowing about Dickie. Spike had always kept his relationships hidden, keeping the truth about his other children from everyone, even his own mother. It wasn't until Miss Pearl learned about

Dickie's existence that the full weight of everything hit her. The secrets Spike had kept from everyone had caused so much pain and confusion.

Miss Pearl couldn't help but feel guilty for not knowing the whole truth, for not understanding just how tangled Spike's life had been. All these years, she had thought she knew everything about her son, but now it seemed like there was so much she had never known.

Spike's devout Christian family had always disapproved of Faye's lifestyle, especially her life of crime. Faye was a booster who stole for a living and taught her kids the same. Dickie and Lawrence had learned how to steal just like their mother, using their young faces as distractions while Faye took what she wanted. It was a life built on deception, and Faye never thought twice about it. But when it came to her children, she would do anything to keep them close.

Faye's anger boiled over one day, and she went to Miss Pearl's house in a fit of rage. With a pistol in her hand, Faye opened fire on Miss Pearl's home. The shots rang out, but none of them hit anyone. Faye wasn't trying to kill anyone—she just wanted to send a message. She wanted her daughter back, and she wasn't going to let anything stop her. But that act of violence sent Faye back to jail, this time for a much longer sentence.

Faye's life was filled with these kinds of moments—outbursts of violence, crime, and chaos. She was always running from the law, always finding ways to avoid the consequences of her actions. But in the end, it was her children who paid the price. Dickie, Lawrence, and Jean Ann were caught in the middle of it all, and they would never escape the cycle of pain, anger, and broken promises.

As the years went on, Dickie would look back on these events with a heavy heart. He would see how everything he had known, everything he had been a part of, was shaped by the choices his mother made, by the family secrets that had been buried for so long. And he would understand, finally, that the life he had lived—tangled in lies and confusion—was not just his own. It was a life marked by the past, mistakes, and choices of the people before him.

And through it all, the question would always remain: What could have been if things had been different? If the family had been whole if the secrets had never been kept, if Faye had made different choices... Could things have turned out differently?

It was April 5, 1953, a Friday afternoon when a fire broke out in the three-story rooming house at 612 Missouri. The night was thick, with a heavy silence as the fire raged through the house. The flames consumed the walls, crackling with a hunger that seemed almost alive, and the air was thick with smoke and desperation. The flames swept through the top floor, causing an estimated $4,500 damage. Neighbors would later say the fire seemed to come out of nowhere, though rumors swirled that Spike had set the fire in retaliation for Faye's shooting up Miss Pearl's house.

Faye, who had always been larger than life, was determined that the fire wouldn't consume her children. Despite the flames around her, she wouldn't let them burn alive. She wasn't a stranger to danger doing what it took to survive. With the fire closing in, Faye tossed her two small children—Lawrence, 4, and Dickie, 2—along with a neighbor's kid, James, 5, out of the third-story window, one by one, to waiting hands below.

Then, in the act of desperate bravery, Faye herself leaped from the burning building, her body landing hard as she fractured her pelvis.

Neighbors rushed to the scene to help, and Faye was later taken to City-County Hospital, her condition initially poor. The fire department was still investigating the cause, though they couldn't confirm if it had been deliberate. The community rallied around Faye and her children in the aftermath, gathering money and supplies. The building, owned by May Turner, would never be the same, and neither would Faye's life after that night.

With Faye gone for what felt like an eternity, Dickie and Lawrence were left behind in a rooming house, a temporary home surrounded by people who didn't know how to care for them. As days turned into weeks and weeks into months, Faye's absence grew longer, and eventually, Dickie and Lawrence were sent to an orphanage. The orphanage was located in Fort Worth, Texas—an area now home to a Walmart on Berry Street. Back then, it was just another small, cramped building where children were sent when no one else could care for them.

The orphanage was a place where Dickie learned to fend for himself. But it wasn't long before the Evans family took Lawrence in, offering him a place in their home. Lawrence wasn't happy about being separated from Dickie, and it didn't take long before he made his move. He ran away. He stole the Evans' car and took off, determined to find his way back to Faye.

Dickie, left alone, felt the sting of abandonment, but he was learning to navigate the world on his own. His mind was sharp, and he began to meet people who told him stories about his family. They spoke of his mother, Lawrence, and the life they had lived before. These stories were like pieces of a puzzle, and Dickie started to see the shape of his life come into focus.

As Dickie continued on this uncertain path, he found a new family. The Wallaces, a couple who lived on the Southside of Fort Worth, took him in, offering him a home and a place in their lives. The Wallaces were no strangers to hard times themselves, but they had a particular way of getting by—one that Dickie would come to understand all too well.

The Wallaces were bootleggers, making and selling illegal alcohol in the dead of night. They were the kind of people who knew how to make money and survive by bending the rules. They saw something in Dickie—a sharpness, a resilience—and decided to raise him as their own. They gave him a new name: Richard Blane Wallace.

Dickie never asked why. He never questioned the name change because it was a chance for him to start over, to live a life that wasn't tangled in the mess of his past. He learned from the Wallaces not just about business but about survival. They taught him how to run things, manage money, and build something out of nothing. It wasn't always easy, but it was real. Dickie became someone who could navigate the world with a certain kind of ease, a confidence that he hadn't known before.

However, the Wallaces weren't perfect. Their involvement in illegal activities shaped Dickie in ways that he couldn't fully understand at the time. They taught him the art of making money, but they also taught him the cost of doing things that weren't always honest. The lessons from the Wallaces shaped the man

Dickie would become—a man who learned the power of both hard work and shortcuts, a man who would one day know how to make his path, even if it meant bending the rules.

But life had a way of coming back around, of pulling the past into the present. After being released from jail, Faye was slowly getting back on her feet. It was during this time that she found out about Dickie's new family. The news hit her hard, and she was far from pleased. She demanded that her child be returned to her, insisting that the Wallaces give Dickie back to her.

There was a deep, tense standoff between Faye and the Wallaces. They had their own history with her, built on bootlegging and the kind of survival that didn't ask questions. Faye wasn't the kind of woman to take no for an answer, and the Wallaces weren't the kind of people to give up what they had worked for. The clash was inevitable, filled with anger, frustration, and resentment.

The tension between Faye and the Wallaces wasn't just about who would raise Dickie. On the other hand, Lawrence found his way back to Faye after running away from the Evan's family. It wasn't just about the kids; it was about the secrets, the lies, and all the messy relationships that had built up over time.

Faye wanted to be the one in charge, who made the decisions. She was their mother, after all. But the Wallaces had become Dickie's family, and they weren't going to let him go without a fight.

Faye's situation was challenging because of her past and lack of resources. She worked as a maid, whereas Mrs. Wallace also worked as a maid for a wealthy white lawyer who lived in White Settlement, a wealthy neighborhood in Fort Worth where only white people lived. In the 1950s, black people could only work in places like White Settlement, but they couldn't live there. They spent their days cleaning and cooking in the homes of wealthy white families.

Seeing Mrs. Wallace's situation, the lawyer helped her adopt Dickie legally. Because of his connections, she was able to give Dickie a new name and a fresh start. This was a big help for her but also brought some problems with her and Faye. The lawyer's help meant that Dickie was now legally connected to the Wallaces, who were now a big part of his life. This made things difficult for Faye, and she didn't know how to fix it since she had no money or way to fight for Dickie's future.

The conflict would grow over time, simmering beneath the surface, but in the end, Dickie was left in the middle, caught between two families who both had claims to him, both had histories with him. He had to make a choice, though the choice was never easy, and the lines between right and wrong were never as clear as they seemed.

As Dickie looked back on those years, he realized that his life had always been about balance. Between his mother's chaotic world and the Wallaces' complicated world of bootlegging and survival, he had learned to walk a fine line. It wasn't the kind of life everyone could understand, but it was the life that had shaped him. And in the end, it was the only life he knew.

After spending years connecting the dots, Dickie now decided to leave Texas and head to California. He wasn't sure exactly what he was running toward, but he knew he needed a fresh start. He arrived in California with big dreams, hoping to find his place in the world.

The glitzy lights of Hollywood were a stark contrast to the life he had known. Dickie soon found himself immersed in the fast-paced world of entertainment, a world that was all about fame, fortune, and flash. He had always been the person who could adapt to any situation, and the comedy scene in California seemed like the perfect fit. Dickie made connections with big names, including Smokey Robinson, and rubbed elbows with some of the most famous figures in show business. The lifestyle was exhilarating—parties, lights, and laughter.

But as the days turned into months, the glamour of California began to wear thin. The fast lifestyle didn't sit well with him. It was empty in a way that no amount of fame could fill. Dickie realized that this wasn't the life he wanted. It wasn't who he was. He needed something more solid, something with purpose.

So, he made a decision. He joined the Marine Corps, which shocked many who had seen him chasing fame on the comedy circuit. But for Dickie, it was a necessary change. The discipline, structure, and clarity of purpose were what he needed to ground himself. The Marine Corps taught him more than he had expected: focus, responsibility, and a sense of self that had been missing from his chaotic upbringing.

But California wasn't done with him yet.

Out of the blue, Dickie had a reunion with someone he hadn't seen in years: his sister, Jean Ann. The reunion was supposed to be a moment of joy, a chance to reconnect with a family member he'd lost touch with. But the meeting wasn't like what Dickie had imagined. Jean Ann didn't want anything to do with their mother, Faye. Raised by Spike's wife, Jean Ann had been taught to hate their mother, a bitterness that ran deep within her.

As soon as they met, Dickie saw it—Jean Ann wasn't just bitter; she was a mirror of Faye. Despite being raised by Spike's wife, Jean Ann cursed and looked just like her mother. She had the same fiery temper, the same sharp tongue, and the same defiance. It was as if their family's cycle had continued despite all attempts to break it. Jean Ann, with all her anger, was Faye in a younger body, acting out in ways that mirrored her mother's struggles.

This revelation shocked Dickie. It was as though he was seeing history repeat itself, but this time in a new generation. No matter how much Jean Ann tried to distance herself from Faye's influence, she was still trapped in the same cycle of dysfunction.

The cycle didn't end with Jean Ann. As time passed, her children—Elaine and JD—entered the story. When they visited their grandmother, Miss Pearl, in Fort Worth, it seemed like a chance for everyone to reconnect. However, Faye soon learned that her grandkids, whom she had never met, were being mistreated and didn't have enough food to eat. Concerned for their well-being, Faye invited the kids to stay with her so she could ensure they were fed and cared for.

But once again, the shadows of the past wouldn't stay hidden. Faye was determined not to let them return to California. Memories flooded back of how Miss Pearl had taken Jean Ann as a child. Faye couldn't shake the feeling that history might repeat itself, and she believed Elaine and JD needed to be raised in Fort Worth, where she could keep a closer eye on them.

Faye felt her responsibility was to protect her grandchildren and provide them with a stable home, even if it meant standing up against her daughter.

Dickie, as usual, found himself stuck in the middle. He tried to help his mother and sister get along, hoping he could fix the distance between them. But Jean Ann's anger towards Faye was too intense. Faye never showed any hatred towards her daughter. She didn't talk about it much, which made Dickie know that she was hurt. Faye didn't seem angry, but he could tell she had been hurt for a long time.

Faye always hoped that Jean Ann would return and take the kids herself, hoping it would help them reconnect. But Jean Ann's anger was too deep, and it was something Dickie couldn't change. Every time he tried, it felt like the problem got worse. The anger between them was like a wall that no one could tear down.

Meanwhile, Lawrence—Dickie's brother—was continuing his tumultuous life. The years hadn't been kind to him. He had spent much of his time in and out of jail, each time returning to the same destructive patterns. But Dickie, even with all his own struggles, was always there for Lawrence. Every time Lawrence called from jail, Dickie was the one who answered. The calls were often filled with desperation and regret, but Dickie never turned his back on him. Lawrence needed him, and Dickie never abandoned his brother, no matter how difficult it was.

But as time passed, Dickie received a call that shook him to his core. Lawrence was dead. He had been found in his home by their younger brother, Michael. Dickie's heart broke as he processed the news. He had always been there for Lawrence, always tried to help him find a way out of his self-destructive cycle, but now it was too late. The reality of how deeply entrenched their family was in dysfunction hit Dickie harder than anything he had ever faced.

As much as Dickie tried to change the path his family was on, as much as he tried to break the cycle, he realized something painful. Some things couldn't be fixed. His family was beyond repair with all its broken pieces and messy histories.

Despite this, Dickie didn't give up on his own life. He had made something of himself. Through all the chaos and all the setbacks, he had found success in business and entrepreneurship. He had learned from the Wallaces, his own experiences, and the hard lessons life had taught him. He had built a life for himself that was stable, successful, and far removed from the turmoil that defined his childhood.

But even with all his success, Dickie couldn't escape the shadow of his family's dysfunction. His mother's passing didn't bring the closure he had hoped for. Instead, it left him with a lingering sense of loss, of things that had never been resolved. He knew that no matter how hard he tried, there would always be a part of him that would never entirely escape the path his family had set before him.

In the end, Dickie accepted the painful truth: he could never entirely change the course of his family's history. No matter how much he tried fixing it, some things were beyond repair.

But he was determined to keep moving forward, to live a life that was his own, no matter the past.

Smoky Robinson and Uncle Dickie

Chapter Three

Bonds Without Blood

In the absence of a father's warmth, children learn to shape their own destinies.

One story my Uncle Michael, my mother's brother, told me sticks in my mind. He remembers when Momma first found out she was pregnant. It was a tough time; he was outside with his girlfriend when Momma came running out of the house, crying and shouting that she was pregnant. Uncle Michael said that moment really stuck with him—not just because of the news, but because it felt like everything was falling apart. She was only sixteen.

By then, my grandmother was working hard, balancing jobs as a maid for white families and doing "at-home health" work. She was always busy, and

Uncle Michael felt like she somehow knew something big would happen with Momma soon. Years before Momma got pregnant, she had promised herself that she would have kids so that her mother could enjoy the presence of grandkids who lived close by.

<u>Momma and Uncle Michael</u>

On January 17, 1978, the night Kevin was born, Fort Worth was very cold. The temperatures dropped below freezing, and light snow fell, making the roads slippery. While it was chilly outside, everything was moving quickly inside the hospital.

Momma lay in the hospital bed, looking determined despite the pain on her face. She gritted her teeth but didn't give up. She was ready to meet her first child. For a moment, her mind wandered back to her younger days, remembering her mother sitting in her chair, wiping away tears after Uncle Dickie moved his kids to California. Grama was heartbroken, and Momma had watched as part of their family slipped away.

"I'll have kids for her," she promised herself. "I'll give my momma grandkids." Even as a teenager, she knew she had to do this. Now, at sixteen, she was about to keep that promise. Kevin was more than just a baby; he symbolized hope, a promise fulfilled.

As she prepared to bring Kevin into the world, memories of his father, Miller Junior, came flooding back. In high school, she spent much time at his house after school. While others went home, she would sneak out to see him; he was her first love. Miller Junior was popular on the south side of Fort Worth, and their relationship felt exciting and innocent. But now, as she lay there, she felt his absence. He wasn't there to hold her hand or offer encouragement. Still, she pushed those thoughts aside; she had her baby, and that was all that mattered.

Finally, Kevin cried out, and Momma felt a rush of love as she held him close. Despite the pain and the storm outside, she felt peace. She promised herself that Kevin would never feel lonely.

Life in their small apartment in the projects became hard as time passed. The walls, floors, and stairs were thick and made of concrete, and the outside of the building was covered in red brick. Unfortunately, the neighbors were often loud, filling the halls with noise and making it challenging to find any peace in their homes. But Grama made it feel like home. After Kevin was born, Momma continued to party and got involved in things she shouldn't have. Uncle Michael noticed changes in her, sensing that she had started using I.V. drugs. It was a shadow that would affect her health later.

Kevin grew up fast, taking on responsibilities that no child should bear. He became the family's protector, watching over Momma and trying to keep her spirits up. When other siblings were born, he stepped in even more, helping with everything and trying to hold the family together.

He often thought about his father, Miller Junior, and promised himself that he wouldn't be like him. He would always be there for his family.

A little over a year after Kevin was born, Momma was back in the same hospital room, getting ready to have her second child, Kasey. It was February 24, 1979—just as cold as the night Kevin was born. This time, however, there was a mix of anxiety and excitement in the air. His father was a man named Marvel, and everyone was surprised by how scared Marvel seemed around Momma. Momma could be intimidating; she once chased a boyfriend around his car with a butcher knife because he looked at another girl. Those moments marked their lives, filled with tension but also showing her strong spirit.

As Kasey's arrival approached, the life cycle continued, bringing new beginnings while reminding them of past struggles. Each moment was part of our family story, a tale of love, resilience, and the challenges of growing up in a world that often felt out of control.

Momma, now seventeen, was still very young but already caring for two kids. She was supposed to be the grown-up but had lost her way somewhere. This time, she wasn't alone—Kasey's father, a quiet man, was with her. He wasn't like the other guys Momma had been with. He wasn't sure of himself. She was light-skinned, and guys liked her—she was used to getting attention. It surprised him when she flirted with him, but he had no idea what would happen next.

Momma didn't care. She was out of control, partying while she should have been taking care of her family. She never learned how to balance things—to give herself entirely to one thing when so many things were pulling at her.

Kasey's birth wasn't the same as Kevin's. Momma was happy, but there was something different about it—a fear, an unease. Kasey's father wasn't emotionally there, and Momma was already distracted. She couldn't figure out how to handle everything—her kids, the men in her life, and the things she wanted for herself.

With Kasey's birth, Kevin had to take on even more responsibility. He wasn't always sure how much he really understood about being the older brother, but he felt the weight of that role. With his dark skin and serious expression, Kasey looked much like his father.

He was quieter and often kept to himself, sneaking around the apartment instead of joining in on the playful chaos that filled the home.

This behavior created tension between Kasey and Grama. She didn't fully trust him, and he reminded her of Uncle Lawrence, who had previously caused problems. Grama's protective instincts kicked in, and she often watched Kasey closely, worried that he might follow in his uncle's footsteps.

Kevin noticed the strain this put on their family. He wanted to help Kasey feel more included and loved but understood Grama's concerns. He tried to bridge the gap between them, encouraging Kasey to join in family activities while reassuring Grama that Kasey was just a little boy trying to find his place. Kasey didn't smile much, partly because of the way his teeth were shaped, which made him appear even more serious. Kevin noticed that Kasey watched everything around him with cautious curiosity as if he were trying to figure out the world. Kevin wanted to make sure

Kasey felt safe and loved, even with the challenges they faced.

As the days turned into weeks, Kevin took it upon himself to look after Kasey, guiding him through the small project apartment and the noise of their neighbors. He wanted to show Kasey that they were a family even in their challenging situation, and he would always be there for him. Kevin often found himself talking to Kasey, sharing stories about their lives, hoping to coax a smile from his little brother. Even though Kasey didn't respond much, Kevin believed that deep down, he understood the bond they shared.

Kevin's childhood was all about responsibility. He learned early on that he had to hold things together. His father was never there, but he didn't act out or seek attention. Instead, he became the strong, dependable one everyone turned to, even without asking.

But deep down, Kevin was tired. Tired of being the adult when he was still just a kid. He was tired of carrying the weight of things that weren't his fault. Tired of wanting approval from a man who couldn't give it. But Kevin kept going. It was what he did.

Whereas Momma was trying to give her best as a mother, despite her struggles with addiction, it wasn't always easy. She had so many things pulling her attention—Kasey, the younger child, who needed her care, and Kevin, who was starting to carry his quiet burdens. Momma wanted to be there for both of them, to support and guide them, but sometimes she couldn't manage it all.

The weight of everything around her—her struggles, her responsibilities, and the chaos of life—often overshadowed the joy of having kids. There were moments when she would look at Kasey and Kevin and feel a rush of love, but her challenges made it hard to enjoy those moments fully. She wanted to laugh and play with them, to create happy memories, but her addiction pulled her in the other direction, leaving her feeling drained and overwhelmed.

Kevin noticed this change in Momma and felt concern and sadness. He wanted her to be happy and to enjoy their time together, but he also understood that she was fighting a difficult battle. Being so young, Kasey sensed the tension but didn't fully understand it. All he knew was that sometimes Momma seemed distant, making him feel unsure.

Life didn't get easier after my arrival. On April 29, 1980, I (Randy) was born. Momma was now eighteen, no longer the young, wide-eyed teenager she had been when she first became a mom. She had already faced so much with Kevin and Kasey and the challenges of being a single mother. Yet here she was, about to welcome another child. This time, though, it felt different. There was no excitement or joy like when Kevin was born, and not even the nervous hope that came with Kasey. My birth felt quieter.

The father was Randolph, who had been trying to talk to Momma for a while. One time, he was in the house with her while Grama was at work, and my Uncle Michael told him, "We can't have company." Uncle Michael wasn't trying to let anything happen, but eventually, I guess it did, and that's how I came to be.

As Momma lay in the hospital alone, her heart felt heavy again. She seemed to accept that being a single mom wouldn't get easier; it would only get harder. Meanwhile, I was born with jaundice and had to stay in the hospital for several days. Momma visited me every day, but it was hard for her. She had to leave me behind, and after everything she had been through, this was just one more challenge to face.

By the time I came in the picture, Momma had moved from Grama's apartment at 509 West Bluff to a new place down the street at 606 West Bluff after remodeling the project building. The walls were still thick, which meant she couldn't hang up pictures, and there was always tension in the air, but it was a step up from where we had been. Even with these small victories, life never truly felt stable.

Things were supposed to be better now. Kevin, still the reliable oldest child, continued living with Grama. The weight of responsibility never left him. Even though he was older, he wasn't ready to leave Grama's house. He continued to shoulder the burden of looking after Kasey and me. Kevin wanted to help Momma as much as possible but also felt the pressure of growing up too fast.

Life was complicated, and the challenges seemed to keep piling on. Kevin often found himself torn between wanting to support Momma and the need to focus on his own life. He loved his siblings but sometimes wished he could just be a kid without all the responsibilities weighing on his shoulders.

As I grew, it became clear that my role in the family differed from Kevin's and Kasey's. Kevin, the older, more serious one, had always been the protector, holding everything together. With his sneaky personality, Kasey was serious, always covering his mouth when smiling or not smiling at all and avoiding Grama at all costs. But I was still trying to figure out where I fit in. Caught between the responsible Kevin and sneaky Kasey, I often felt unsure of my place.

I was always quiet, watching from the sidelines, unsure of where I fit in. Even though Kevin was older and was always responsible for taking care of the family, he wasn't always easy to talk to. He grew up too fast, carrying burdens no child should have to.

It's hard to explain what it feels like to be stuck between two worlds. I wasn't like Kevin, as well as Kasey. Maybe it was Momma's soft side that I inherited, or perhaps it was just how everything felt so raw in my heart, but I often sensed that I was too sensitive for my world. When things went wrong, I felt it intensely. It wasn't just the big moments that affected me, but the small ones too.

For Momma, each child was a reminder of her promises to herself and others—promises that got harder to keep as life became more difficult. She wasn't the mom she had hoped to be when she was younger. Raising three kids, each with their own needs, was overwhelming. Sometimes, it felt like she was walking through life in a fog, trying to make the best of a situation that wasn't what she had imagined. But she kept going because there was no other choice.

I could feel the tension when Momma and Uncle Michael fought, their voices raised and filled with frustration. It hurt to see them clash, and I wished for peace. Then there was Kevin, who would stand there looking serious and distant, carrying a weight that no one his age should have to bear. I could see the burden on his shoulders and wished I could lighten his load somehow.

And then there was Kasey, sneaking food out of the refrigerator, blaming me when he got caught, and leading us all to a whooping. I felt the sting of the punishment, not just on my body but in my heart, because I knew I hadn't done anything wrong. In those moments, I wished for understanding and connection, but instead, I often felt alone in my sensitivity. It was as if I lived in a world filled with noise and chaos, while my heart longed for calm and kindness.

Even though I tried to be there for everyone—smoothing things over and trying to keep the peace—I never knew how to fix myself. I often felt like I didn't fit in, as if I were always waiting for something, but I didn't even know what that was.

Then there was the thing with my dad. Or, really, the lack of a dad. The person I knew as my father, Randolph Dawkins, was someone I longed to have a relationship with. I still have a letter from him while he was in jail, promising to come hang out with me; one day he promised to take me to Six Flags. I was so excited that I couldn't sleep. I dressed and sat on the porch early the next morning, waiting for him. This was later in life, years after we moved from the projects. My brothers walked past, asking, "He still not here?" and laughed, saying, "He ain't coming." Sure enough, I sat there all day, and he never showed up. I felt mostly embarrassed, realizing how foolish it was to think he would do anything for me when he had never done anything before that.

I don't remember the first time I realized I didn't know who my real dad was. I was too young to ask, but I sensed something was wrong. Momma would always talk about him, even taking me to meet his grandmother one day. When Momma introduced us, she said, "Oh my, I didn't know Ran could have kids." That stuck with me as a child.

It wasn't until later when I was old enough and after he died at the age of 42, that I submitted DNA to Ancestry.com. Then, I learned the man I thought was my dad wasn't really my dad.

When I found out the truth, it hit me hard. I wasn't angry at first, but I felt something shift inside me.

Everything I thought I knew and felt familiar didn't make sense anymore. I realized I was more different than I thought, and the truth made me feel even more alone, as if I didn't belong anywhere. It was a heavy burden to carry, compounded by the knowledge that I still have no idea who my actual father is, leaving a void in my identity that I struggle to fill.

Then Brandon was born on January 25, 1982. Things moved quickly after that. Uncle Michael had his own things going on, including having a baby on the way with a lady named Donna while Momma was having Brandon. It was hard to keep track of everything at the time, especially with the family growing so fast and so many changes happening.

Momma still didn't have everything figured out. None of us did. And Brandon's dad? Well, he was no different than the others—physically and emotionally absent, leaving Momma to handle everything on her own. By then, we were all used to it. It was just how things were.

Brandon's dad was supposed to be a man named Johnny Brown, AKA JB, but some people said this guy named Duke, who lived in the projects, could be the father, though we didn't know for sure. Brandon first met JB when he was eight and felt no connection to him. He just popped up one day and took Brandon on a long walk to his house, which had to be a very uncomfortable feeling, walking alongside a total stranger.

Later, Momma saw a lady at the store she hadn't seen in years. Momma said Brandon looked like the lady, and since Momma had a relationship with the lady's brother in the past, she concluded that he just had to be Brandon's father. His name was Duke. The guy was in the County Jail. One look at Brandon, and he said, "That ain't mine." He called him "That."

When Brandon was born, Momma seemed to find peace in the chaos. But for me, he was just another baby—another change in our family dynamic that I didn't know how to handle. I was still trying to figure out where I fit in, caught between Kevin, who was serious, and Kasey, who was devious. And now, there was Brandon—sweet and innocent, already trying to find his place in the world.

But Brandon was different. He developed this fire in him, an anger he couldn't explain. Maybe it was because life had been hard on him from the start or because he never had a chance to grow up without struggle. I saw it in him—this need to prove himself to the world, to show everyone he was strong. But deep down, I think he just wanted someone to care about him, see him and tell him he mattered.

Brandon didn't talk much about his childhood, but I saw how he acted out and always had this tough exterior. It wasn't about fitting in with other kids; he joined gangs because he wanted to protect others, to be the strong one, even if it meant building walls that kept everyone else out.

School was hard for him. I could see the frustration on his face, how he would act out when he couldn't keep up, when the work seemed impossible. Nobody really helped him. Nobody noticed how much he was hurting.

It wasn't until he got into juvenile detention that he finally felt someone cared. They listened to him, fed him, gave him clothes, and provided education. For the first time, someone saw him for more than just the tough kid who didn't fit in. And that made him wonder why the people who were supposed to care— Momma and everyone else—didn't give him the attention he needed.

I saw his anger and pain, and I understood it more than he probably realized. I wasn't the tough one, but we were the same inside. We both just wanted to be seen, to matter in a world that made us feel invisible.

Growing up in a place like this was hard. When everything felt broken, knowing where the pieces fit was tough. Kevin, Kasey, and Brandon all had roles and ways of dealing with the world. But me? I was always in between, trying to hold it all together and make sense of a life that never really made sense.

I'm not sure if I'll ever figure it out. But I'm still here, still trying. Still trying to understand who I am and who I've always been.

As the years passed, I saw my brothers find their own paths. Life is funny that way. Even though none of us ever really knew the full story of our fathers, we all found a way to define ourselves. We were shaped by absence, by the love we shared, and by the little pieces of each other we picked up along the way.

Kevin, the oldest, always carried this weight. He didn't show his feelings much, but I could see it in him—the responsibility, the way he tried to hold everything together for us. Even when he was younger, he seemed to have this sense of maturity, like he was the one who had to take care of the rest of us.

Maybe it was because he didn't have a dad to guide him. It was like Kevin felt he had to protect our family, even though he was still just a kid.

Then there was Kasey, who was cunning and was mistreated by our grandmother, but he didn't let things phase him. He didn't let his younger siblings get to him; he would rarely fight us, unlike the way Kevin and I did. I didn't always understand him. He wasn't like me. Like the time I burned him on his leg, or the time I burned him on his cheek, or when I almost decapitated him with a string, he never retaliated.

He didn't seem to feel things as deeply, or maybe he didn't show it. He lived in the moment, and I suppose that was his way of coping with all the hurt we'd grown up with.

But for me? I've always been caught in between. I couldn't be as intimidating as Kasey. I couldn't shoulder the weight the way Kevin did. I was the one who felt the quiet ache of being in the middle. I wanted to stay out of trouble but had the desire to be seen and the need to matter. I was just... different from everyone. We were all shaped by the same absence but responded to it in our own ways.

Then came Leisa, born on December 2nd, 1982—eleven months after Brandon. Another change in the family. Everyone was surprised that Momma had another child so soon, but we were happy to have a little sister on the way. This time, the dad was a man named Lee Duncan. Lee was one of the fathers always around; although he wasn't there financially, he genuinely loved his daughter and was always in her life, much different from the rest of our fathers. For the first time in a long time, there was a sense of joy and hope that things might be better for her. Maybe she would have a life without carrying the same weight we had.

But things didn't go as we had hoped. Leisa's birth was supposed to be the start of something new. But, as often happens, life had other plans. The truth is,

Momma was never the same after Leisa was born. She had to have a C-section, just like with all of us, but this time, there were problems. What was supposed to be a simple procedure turned into a scary situation when she hemorrhaged afterward. The doctors told my grandmother that she needed a hysterectomy—if she didn't have it, she would have died. But thank God, her life was spared.

Even though Momma survived, the experience took a huge toll on her. She was left feeling weak and exhausted, and the stress of her struggles grew. With Leisa in the world, we all hoped she could escape the cycle that had trapped our family.

Leisa was our little sister, and we all needed to look out for her. But as she grew up, she eventually followed the same path as our mother and grandmother. Momma traded one drug for another, although while she wasn't using I.V. drugs anymore, crack cocaine came into the picture. The crack epidemic of the 1980s and 1990s brought serious problems, flooding our neighborhood with addiction and crime. Families were torn apart, and many lives were changed forever by this powerful drug. It was a tough reality that we all knew too well, and it hung over us like a dark cloud. As the crack epidemic affected our lives, it became clear that Leisa would have to face the same challenges we all had.

It was painful to watch. Leisa, our bright spot, now seemed caught in the same troubles that had affected our family for so long. The cycle felt unbreakable, and as we looked out for her, we couldn't help but worry that she might end up on the same path as Momma and Grama despite our efforts. It felt like fate had already cast its shadow over her life, and we could only hope that somehow, she would find a way to rise above it.

My family went through a lot through all this, but there was always love and care for one another. Even though things were hard, we stuck together. Our family survived and kept moving forward, no matter what. Whenever we faced a new challenge or hit another roadblock, we found a way to keep going — together.

Randy (far left), Kasey (middle), Kevin (far right), Brandon (bottom)

Chapter Four

The Blue Bicycle

Childhood is not defined by the memories we cherish but by the scars we carry and the stories they unfold.

They say the past is never really gone; it's just waiting to come back. One night, I found myself thinking about how things were before I came along — the constant moving and the search for something that always seemed out of reach. Uncle Michael often talked about their journey, bouncing from place to place, never staying long enough to put down roots.

First, it was the South Side of Fort Worth. Uncle Michael described it as a close community where neighbors looked out for one another. I never really understood this until I moved there as a kid. Suddenly, the neighborhoods where my mother had grown up became my own home, filled with stories and memories of my family's past. I began to see the streets, parks, and houses through a new lens, connecting with the history that shaped my family and discovering what it meant to be part of that community.

After the South Side, they moved to Poly, where they found a small house on Wallace Street. But stability didn't last long. Uncle Michael told me about a big argument between Grama and the landlord that ended their hopes of staying there. Soon enough, they were back on the South Side, stuck in that tiring cycle of searching for a place to belong. That feeling of never having a true home always stuck with me—the sense that they were always moving, never really fitting in anywhere.

Then came Eastwood, where they lived in a house on Wyman Street for about a year. I wasn't born yet, but Uncle Michael had plenty of stories to share. He would tell me about the carport they had there, which seemed like a big deal until one stormy night when it collapsed onto Uncle Dickie's car while he was visiting from California. Uncle Michael said Dickie was really angry, especially since the landlord wouldn't take responsibility. Tensions rose again, and soon they were packing up to move once more.

Their next stop was Berryhill, where they stayed only briefly before finally moving into the projects—where they would spend the longest time. It was there, in that rough and unfamiliar place, that Uncle Michael's memories became clearer. He remembered being around nine or ten when they moved in, right when he started fifth grade. That was when everything began to change for their family—Grama started drinking more, Momma began partying, and Uncle Michael found himself trying to hold it all together. He played basketball, flirted with girls, but always kept an eye on his family, feeling the weight of responsibility grow heavier each day.

Even as a kid, Uncle Michael had to step up in ways no one else did. He would wait for Grama to come home from the club, making sure she got back safe, watching over her, even when he was just a boy himself.

Then, Momma started having more kids, and eventually, Uncle Michael had kids too. His first child was with my Aunt Donna, whom he ended up marrying. But things didn't work out between them because Uncle Michael felt like he was being pushed into a life he wasn't ready for. He eventually got a job, but most of his paycheck went to child support, so money was tight.

Always thinking ahead, Momma suggested to Grama that we all move in together. So, we did—another change, but this time it felt like we were trying to find some stability, even if it meant staying closer as a family.

We moved out of the projects to the South Side, a place that was very familiar to Uncle Michael and my mother. First, we settled into a big green house on

Jessamine Street. We all lived there for a while, but eventually, we moved to a smaller house on Powell Street.

From Jessamine to Powell, and then to a big brown house on Polinski Street. The house on Polinski was two stories, with two rooms upstairs and several rooms downstairs. Grama had her own room, and Uncle Michael and Momma each had their own rooms. The kids shared a room in the back of the house. There was also a playroom. It was a big house, and we enjoyed it, but things got tough, and eventually, we were evicted.

After that, we ended up in a house on Humboldt. It felt like we were always moving, always searching for something better. This was also when a man named Chatney came into the picture with Momma. By this time, she couldn't have any more kids, so they never had any together. The house on Humboldt was actually vacant, and Chatney noticed it was empty, so we all moved in.

During this time, Uncle Michael met a lady named Mary, who already had one child named Nicholas and had just delivered Uncle Michael's second child, Julius. Chatney was the kind of guy who could quickly get into Momma's head, telling her to do shady things like swatting. So, we lived in the house on Humboldt: Grama, Uncle Michael, Mary, Momma, Chatney, and seven kids—Kevin, Kasey, Randy, Brandon, Leisa, Nicholas, and Julius. Apparently, Momma was trying to get more money out of Mary, and Uncle Michael asked her, "Why are you trying to get money out of her? Nobody is paying rent, and the owner didn't even know we were living here."

That's when the big fight happened while we were living on Humboldt. It had something to do with Momma and Chatney, and things got really heated. Uncle Michael wanted to confront Chatney, but Momma wouldn't let him. Chatney went to get his brother, and then they all got into it. Momma told Uncle Michael that he had to leave, and Grama told her, "If he isn't going to be here, then I'm not going to be here." So, they both left. This shocked all of us. I don't really remember this part, but Kevin remembers it vividly; he later asked, "After all the things Grama has done to hold this family together, how does her daughter kick her out?"

But we are family, and it just so happened that Grama started receiving her Social Security check and found a house on Tucker Street. The tension had settled by then and Momma eventually moved in with her, and we then moved to Illinois Street before settling on Stewart Street. I don't remember much about that time, but I do remember the big move to Stewart Street, which is where the blue bicycle comes in. That was one of the moments when I knew our family was changing again.

I remember waking up one morning with sunlight pouring through the window. I stretched and rubbed my eyes, scratching my body—my signature sign that I was still sleepy and a bit groggy. Then, I saw it. Right beside the door was a shiny blue bicycle, the kind you don't see anymore. It had a banana seat and big handlebars. A mix of confusion, excitement, and a hint of being lost washed over me as I took in the sight of it.

I had no idea where it came from. I was eight years old, and my mind raced with possibilities. I thought it had to be a gift from my father. He wasn't really around, but I convinced myself that maybe, just maybe, he had shown up out of nowhere and left me this gift.

But as the years went by, I wondered if I was wrong. I never really found out where that bike came from. Not until much later.

It was in my forties when I finally learned the truth. I was visiting my older brother Kevin, now incarcerated, and I casually mentioned that story, about the bike I thought my father had given me. He looked at me, puzzled, and asked, "What are you talking about? I got you that bike."

It hit me like a ton of bricks. My brother—quiet, always in the background—had been the one to get me that bike. Not my dad. I'd spent years thinking I had been given something special by someone who wasn't there, but the real gift had come from my brother.

The realization brought me a strange sense of peace. It made me look at things differently, like maybe all the pieces of the past were just waiting for the right moment to fit together. And it was this moment—this strange realization—made me want to write down my story. To try to understand how we all saw the same things, but in different ways.

Thinking back on that bike, though, I couldn't help but let my mind wander further, past the bike, back to some of those memories that didn't always make sense at the time.

I remembered the dream I had when I was little. I was in the downtown projects, and in the dream, I saw the Incredible Hulk. I swear, it felt real like I could touch him. But when I told anyone about it, they just looked at me like I was crazy.

Then there was Kasey, my other brother. I once saw him standing at an upstairs window in the projects, yelling at someone. I remember the moment so clearly, but what stood out more was how my mind started plotting ways to get back at him. I had a long memory, and I wasn't above revenge.

One memory that still sticks with me is when Kevin and Kasey tricked me into drinking what I thought was lemonade. I was young but knew something wasn't right when the taste hit my tongue. It was... urine. I could never forget that feeling.

In retaliation, I came up with a plan. I decided that when Kasey was standing at that window, I'd sneak up behind him and burn him with a hot iron on the back of his leg. It was childish and cruel, but it felt like the only way to get back at him at that time.

Those days were filled with small, strange moments, little bits of mischief and memories that didn't seem to fit together until much later. I could almost see the pieces—like my childhood self-trying to make sense of the chaos.

As I began to write this book, memories from my past pulled me in different directions, making it hard to focus on just one. But then something came back to me—something that struck me with a strange kind of heaviness.

I remember when I was about ten years old, and I asked my mom about the scar on my forehead. I had no recollection of how it happened but had seen it in the mirror all my life. She told me it was from when I was three. She had been in a really bad moment, she said, and lost her temper. She had thrown me down the concrete stairs in the downtown projects, 606 West Bluff. The harshness of those steps and the way the blood had run down my head made her feel sad, but she never took me to the hospital. I didn't know what to say to that. How could someone hurt their own child like that? I didn't know whether to feel angry or sad, but somehow, I didn't let it consume me. I had always been sensitive, and that seemed to irritate her more than anything. My mom had a lot of her own demons to fight, and I learned early on that I had to carry some things by myself.

What I do remember, though, is how I ended up living with Grama after that. Grama was always the calm in the storm. She was a steady presence, someone I could count on. It's funny how one person can become a stabilizing force when everything else around you feels like it's falling apart. Grama gave me a sense of comfort, a place where I didn't feel the weight of everything. She was my rock.

When we moved out of the projects to the big green house on Jessamine, life felt like an adventure. Even though we didn't have much, we made do with what we had. We learned to be resourceful, finding joy in the little things. Grama, my mom, and her friend

Mamie would head out to garage sales almost every weekend. They would come back with bags filled with clothes and little trinkets that felt like treasures to us.

I remember hand-me-downs from Kevin, and how they never quite fit right but still felt like a gift. It was a strange kind of comfort, knowing that we didn't have everything, but we had enough. We had each other.

And then there was the Atari. I'll never forget those nights. We'd crowd around the TV, the screen flickering as we repeatedly played Pac-Man, Asteroids, and Space Invaders. It wasn't the newest system, but it didn't matter. It was our world, our escape. For a while, it felt like we could forget everything else. The world outside faded as we pressed buttons and tried to beat high scores.

Mamie, though, was different. She wasn't just a family friend—she was more like a mother to Kevin. She always looked out for us, especially Kevin. She also had an adopted son, Monte, who I envied as he seemed to have all the newest games, shoes, and toys. Mamie cared for him, and Monte and Kevin developed a brotherly bond. I often wondered why she favored Kevin so much, and wondered if I had someone like her in my life earlier, perhaps my path would have been different.

But I was just a kid, and sometimes, I let my curiosity get the better of me.

One day, when I was about six or seven, my curiosity got the best of me, and I did something I shouldn't have. I found a newspaper and, in a moment of childish wonder, decided to set it on fire. At first, it seemed harmless, just a little flame flickering. But before I knew it, the fire grew quickly and started to scare me. I rushed to the sink, hoping to put it out, but it was filled with Grama's chicken soaking in water, getting ready for dinner. In my panic, I ended up tossing the burning paper into the trash. What I thought was a simple mistake turned into a bigger problem as the flames began to spread, reminding me that my curiosity had serious consequences.

I didn't know what I'd done until Uncle Lawrence caught a whiff of the smoke. I still remember his deep voice shouting, "I smell something burning." I acted like I didn't know what was going on, but he wasn't fooled. My heart raced as he grabbed that trash can and threw it outside. I was scared to death. Uncle Lawrence wasn't a man to mess with. His presence was enough to make anyone freeze in their tracks. Standing at 6'5" and weighing about 250 pounds, Uncle Lawrence was a mountain of a man, dark as night with muscles that seemed to ripple beneath his shirt. His size alone could intimidate, and when he spoke, you knew not to argue.

He had a temper like no other. I remember the time he tied a noose and threatened to hang one of us from the basketball goal. The fear in my chest felt like a weight I couldn't shake off. Uncle Lawrence wasn't just tough; he was unpredictable. He had a dark side, and everyone knew it. I remember him dragging his girlfriend down the hall once, stomping on her face with his converse tennis shoes. That image is still burned into my memory.

It wasn't just the violence that scared me, though. It was how he could flip from a threat to a joke in a split second. One minute, he'd be joking, and the next, he'd be towering over us, telling us how he was going to "kill" us. It wasn't a joke anymore. We learned to fear him, to keep our distance, and to stay out of his way. Despite all his threats and scare tactics, Uncle Lawrence never actually hurt us. His intimidation was enough to make us obey, but deep down, we knew that was all it was—fear without follow-through.

But through all that, life moved on, and I found myself here—writing this book, in the present, reflecting on how far I'd come. The cool breeze from the open window felt strange against my skin, grounding me in the moment. As I stared at the computer screen, I couldn't help but wonder about the paths I had taken, my choices, and how each experience shaped who I am today. What lessons had I learned along the way? How would my story resonate with others who have faced their own challenges? The questions swirled in my mind, urging me to dive deeper into the memories that had brought me to this point.

The more I thought about it, the more it seemed like there had to be a reason for all the things that had happened. Or maybe it wasn't a grand plan at all. Maybe life just worked that way. Maybe the memories and struggles were just what shaped us, whether we liked it or not.

As I sat there, lost in thoughts about my past, a siren suddenly blared from down the street, snapping me back to reality. My mind raced back to that night when I was about ten or eleven, and the sirens echoed in my ears. At first, they seemed distant, but they quickly grew louder and closer, filling the air with an unsettling urgency.

Uncle Lawrence had been acting strangely in the days leading up to that night—distant and unpredictable, as if he were a storm brewing on the horizon. I remember feeling a mix of confusion and anxiety; something felt off. When the police finally showed up outside, a realization clicked inside me. I didn't fully grasp the details back then, but deep down, I knew it had something to do with him.

The flashing lights illuminated our front yard, casting eerie shadows that danced across the ground. I could see the officers moving swiftly, their serious expressions adding to the tension in the air. It was as if my childhood innocence was being stripped away, replaced by a gnawing awareness of the complexities of life and the dangers lurking just beyond our doorstep. That night would forever be etched in my memory, a pivotal moment that connected my past with the uncertainty of the present.

Chapter Five

The Last Goodbye

The past may shape us, but it does not have to define us.

I stood outside our old house on Stewart Street, feeling a strange mix of nostalgia and nervousness. Memories of our years on this street flooded back—friends like Big Fish and Bootsy, afternoons spent playing street football, and the unforgettable night Uncle Lawrence ran from the police.

As I walked through the house, more memories began to rush back. I could almost hear Grama's voice, smell her cooking coming from the kitchen, and feel the warmth of the moments we shared. Uncle Lawrence's loud burps and the crunch of a jalapeño pepper—both of which still annoy me—echoed in my mind. Yet, even amidst the chaos of life, these sounds reminded me of happier times.

I kept moving through the rooms, letting the memories guide me. When I reached the back room, the smallest one in the house, I remembered how it had once been a closet until Mr. Turner, the landlord, enlarged it to give me my own space. But now, the house felt different—just a shell of its former self.

As I think back to that night when the sirens blared, I can still feel the tension in the air. It was the night a crime happened just down the street. I was only ten or eleven, but the memory is as clear as day. We were outside, enjoying the cool night air and playing in the front yard when, out of nowhere, the wailing sound of sirens filled the silence.

At first, I thought it might be just an accident or maybe a robbery nearby. But then I looked up and saw police helicopters swirling above, their bright lights cutting through the darkness. The neighborhood that had always felt like a safe haven suddenly transformed into something frightening, like a scene from a movie about a war zone.

People rushed out of their houses, their faces filled with worry and confusion. I could hear snippets of conversation, whispers about what might be happening. My heart raced, caught between curiosity and fear, as I watched from a distance. That night changed everything for me; it was the moment I realized that danger could invade even the safest places.

Then I saw Uncle Lawrence. He was walking down the street, calm as ever, when he spotted the police cars pulling up. His eyes grew wide. Without a word, he turned and ran, disappearing around the corner. At the time, I didn't understand why. I didn't know about the dangers he faced, about how the police often treated Black men like him. I didn't realize that, just by running, he might have made things worse. But

I could see the fear in his eyes, the panic that drove him to escape.

The police surrounded the house, and for hours, it felt like everything was on hold. I watched from the window, my heart racing as my excitement turned into something darker. I learned later that for many Black men, encounters with law enforcement can be filled with fear and uncertainty. They often have to navigate a world where they are seen as threats rather than individuals. That night, I began to grasp the weight of that reality.

Years later, I found myself in a similar situation when the police came looking for my brother Kasey. The memory of that night came rushing back as I watched the police surround our home once again. The same feelings of fear and confusion washed over me.

Uncle Lawrence was used to situations like this; after all, he was a big Black guy with a criminal background, and he often seemed guilty even when he wasn't. He had spent more time in jail than free, which shaped how he saw the world. He was always a bit different, but in a way that made him unforgettable.

One of his strange habits was his strong dislike for what he called "bird baths"—those quick, half-hearted showers where you just wash up without really getting clean. I later learned that this was probably because of his years in prison, where many inmates had to bathe in the sinks of their cells. It was a small detail, but it showed how his past affected him.

More than anything, Uncle Lawrence had a talent for stealing. It wasn't that he was a bad person; it was something he learned from our grandmother. She would always say, "You gotta do what you gotta do to survive." For her, it wasn't about luxury; it was about getting by and making sure you had what you needed when you had nothing. Uncle Lawrence picked up on this lesson early in life, knowing that sometimes you had to take risks to get by.

Despite his flaws, Uncle Lawrence always came through for us when it mattered most. I remember a time when I desperately needed some shoes. I wasn't used to having brand-name sneakers, so when I saw that he had gotten me the new Magic Johnson Converse shoes, I was beyond excited. I had been dreaming of them for months—everyone at school was talking about them, and I wanted to fit in.

However, when I finally slipped them on, I realized he had gotten the wrong size. They were way too small, and I had to curl my toes inside just to wear them. I felt so embarrassed, but I didn't say anything. I knew he couldn't return them for a different size. So, I wore those shoes every day, even though they hurt my feet. As time went on, they began to tear at the seams and started to "talk" with each step. It was a small sacrifice I was willing to make because I wanted to go to school no matter what.

To keep them together, I took super glue and glued the tips of the edges every day before school. But by the end of the day, I found myself walking in ways to hide my feet because my toes and socks were showing.

That was the thing about our family—we didn't have much, but what we had, we made it count. Those shoes were more than just shoes to me. They were a symbol of what we'd gone through, of the struggles and sacrifices we faced just to get by. That experience is why I appreciate so many shoes today; I learned how important it is to feel comfortable and confident in what I wear.

As I thought about those days, the memories of Uncle Lawrence, and the shoes, I couldn't help but wonder about the past, the choices we made, and the struggles we faced.

The move from the White House at 1305 Stewart Street to the Green House at 1327 Stewart Street felt like a huge shift for us. I don't remember it being a smooth transition—nothing in our lives ever really was—but the Green House became a place where we began to rebuild, in a way. The house itself wasn't much—just another cramped space—but it had something the White House didn't: a small house in the back where my mother was able to have her own space while still living close to my grandmother.

Mr. and Mrs. Green were a big part of that. They were kind neighbors—always offering us extra vegetables from their garden or letting us borrow a cup of sugar when we needed it. They were the kind of people who made you feel like the world wasn't all bad. Mr. and Mrs. Green owned both the Green House we were renting and the house next door. At the time, I always thought that only older Black people could be successful, because everyone else I knew was just trying to make it. Mr. and Mrs. Green were one of the only successful Black people I knew. There was also Mr. Turner, who owned the white house, and our house on Ashcresent.

There were days when I'd forget about the weight of our struggles, like when we'd go sledding at Hillside

Park. The laughter, the cold wind biting at my face, and the rush of sliding down the hill—it was the kind of carefree fun I thought I'd left behind. For a while, those moments seemed to erase everything else, if only for a few hours. But as much as I wanted to escape, the truth of our situation always lingered, especially when I'd see my mom battling her addiction. She tried to hide it, but I could always tell when things were getting bad. I remember the way she'd disappear for days at a time, and the way her absence made the house feel quieter, emptier. Poverty had a way of creeping in, too, no matter how many people smiled at us or how much snow we sledded through. It felt like no matter how much light there was, there was always darkness around the corner.

One day, when I was younger, I did something that, looking back, could have turned out a lot worse than it did. I was just being my usual mischievous self, like any kid, but this time it wasn't a simple prank or a harmless mistake. I had found a pipe from the ashtray, and for some reason, I thought it would be fun to mess around with it. I didn't really understand the danger; I guess I was just curious, thinking it was some kind of grown-up toy.

I put the pipe in my mouth, and before I even realized what was happening, I started to choke. Panic set in as the air vanished from my lungs, and my chest felt tight. For a moment, I truly believed I might be in serious trouble. It felt like the walls were closing in on me.

That's when I heard my grandmother's voice cutting through the fear. She was always nearby, keeping a watchful eye on me, almost like a guardian angel. I knew she had a sixth sense for when I was getting into trouble, even if she wasn't right next to me. In a flash, she rushed over, gave me a firm smack on the back, and suddenly, the air rushed back into my lungs. I gasped for breath, tears streaming down my cheeks as I struggled to regain my composure.

I remember her scolding me with a mix of anger and fear. "What did I tell you about putting stuff in your mouth? Don't be a fool. You never know when things can go south." She wasn't just upset; she was scared for me. Her warnings about the dangers of the world echoed in my ears, and in that moment, I understood that she cared deeply for me. I was reckless, and she recognized that. Though I was just a kid, she treated me like I needed to grasp the risks around me.

Her words stuck with me, shaping how I approached life from that day forward. Maybe it wasn't the best way to live, but I became cautious. I learned to think twice before diving into anything. To make matters worse, the pipe I had almost choked on was actually used by my mother and uncles to smoke crack, something I didn't understand at the time. That revelation left my grandmother furious, but I was blissfully unaware of just how dangerous that situation had been.

Not long after that, I learned what crack was and why my mother and uncles acted so strangely. My mom would buy her drugs from a lady who lived down the street from our house on Stewart. At first, she would send Kasey to make the purchases, but one day, Kasey's mischievous behavior made her start using me instead. We would take the money to the lady, and she would give us a matchbox in return. Onetime, Kasey said he lost the money, only to miraculously find it later in the backyard, which is why I was chosen for the task.

One night, while walking home, I decided to open the matchbox, and that's when I saw it—a small, irregularly shaped piece of white, soap-like material. It looked so innocent at first, but as an adult, it infuriates me that I was left to handle something so dangerous. What if I had tasted it? What if I had thought it was candy? I was barely eleven years old, completely unaware of the risks.

Looking back, I realize how careless it was for the adults around me to put me in that situation. The thought of what could have happened still sends chills down my spine. Children shouldn't be exposed to such dangers. It made me realize just how important it is to protect children from such harmful influences, even if the adults in their lives don't fully understand the consequences.

As time passed, things began to shift again. The last time I saw Uncle Lawrence was at a barbecue for my little brother Brandon's homecoming after prison. It was one of those family gatherings that felt both familiar and strange at the same time. Uncle Lawrence was different. There was a change in him that I couldn't quite put my finger on. He wasn't the same man who had run from the cops years ago, always glancing over his shoulder. He seemed lighter, more at ease with himself.

When he looked at me, there was a sense of pride in his eyes that I had never seen before. He said something that has stuck with me through the years: "You're doing good, Randy. I see you making something of yourself. I know I was hard on ya'll, but I'm proud of you."

Hearing those words felt surreal. Uncle Lawrence had always been the rebel, the one who defied the rules, the one who lived on the edge of the law. But now, when I looked into his eyes, I saw something different—something like hope. He shared that he was turning his life around, working on himself, and staying clean. I wanted to believe him. I wanted to believe that the man I had both feared and admired had finally found his way out of the darkness.

His words, simple yet powerful, brought a sense of relief I hadn't realized I needed. They made me rethink everything—how I had viewed Uncle Lawrence and how I had seen our family. I had spent so long clinging to the past, holding onto the pain and unanswered questions, that I hadn't noticed the bigger picture. Maybe Uncle Lawrence wasn't the hero I had hoped for, but he was a survivor. In his own way, he had been trying to teach me how to navigate the struggles of life too.

Uncle Lawrence had always been about survival, about doing whatever it took to get through another day. I felt like I was starting to understand him on a deeper level. The man, the mystery, the family—we weren't as broken as I had once thought. We were just trying to make it, each in our own way, and maybe that was enough.

But then, not long after that barbecue, tragedy struck. Uncle Lawrence passed away suddenly. At that time, he was married and living in the same apartments as my Uncle Michael. When his wife couldn't reach him by phone, she asked Uncle Michael to check on him. To his shock, he found his brother unresponsive on the floor, just steps away from getting out of the shower.

The news hit our family hard, and Uncle Michael was utterly devastated. It didn't make sense. One minute, he was there, talking about how he was changing, and the next, he was gone. His death left behind a hundred unanswered questions. How had he really died? Was it the same old demons that haunted him, or had he been telling the truth? I'll never know.

I wasn't close to Uncle Lawrence, so I didn't feel the emptiness others might have. Instead, I felt the weight of a missed opportunity to get to know him better. At the time, I couldn't attend his funeral or mourn with the family. Even now, I can't help but wonder what stories I never heard, what parts of him I'll never understand. That sense of mystery has stayed with me, lingering in the background, like a question that can never be answered. I still think about him.

I still think about how life can change in the blink of an eye, and how some things we'll never fully understand. But I carry those lessons—those memories of Uncle Lawrence and my grandmother—everywhere

I go. They shaped me in ways I never saw coming, and I carry them, even now.

Uncle Lawrence had always been a complicated figure. His actions—both good and bad—had left behind a trail of confusion, unresolved feelings, and questions. We all had our own versions of him, our own ways of remembering him, and those memories didn't always line up. But the one thing everyone seemed to agree on was that his death had left more questions than answers.

In The Loving Memories Of Uncle Lawerence

Chapter Six

1305 Stewart to 2717 Ashcresent

"You're not ready for what's coming."

I stepped inside my house and closed the door behind me with a sigh. A strange mix of curiosity and nostalgia washed over me as I reflected on everything that had happened in my family. I knew I needed to clear my head, so I headed straight for the bathroom, turning the tap to let the hot water run. The steam began to fill the room, creating a warm cocoon that felt both comforting and isolating.

My mind drifted back to 1991, to a time I had long pushed to the back of my mind. It was a year filled with both joy and pain, a time when everything seemed simpler yet was anything but. I remembered the laughter of family get-togethers, the smell of my grandmother's cooking filling the air, and the warmth of summer days spent playing outside. But alongside those memories were shadows—whispers of conflict and moments of fear that shaped my understanding of the world.

Our family had just moved from 1305 Stewart to 2717 Ashcresent. I still remember how chaotic that time was. Stewart Street was a thrilling yet challenging chapter in our lives. We moved from 1305 to 1327 in an effort to save some money. Believe it or not, we couldn't even afford a moving truck, so we transported all our belongings in a rolling metal shopping cart. Can you picture us struggling to push a mattress in a basket up the street?

We resided at 1327 for a while before returning back to 1305 once more. Our landlord, Mr. Turner, informed my grandmother about a house he had on the other side of town on Ashcresent. It was a much better deal, so we packed up once again and moved. Packing up our lives into a truck felt like a whirlwind.

There was a lot to do, and every room in the house seemed like it was filled with boxes, all piled high and waiting to be sorted. But there was also something exciting about it. The thought of starting fresh in a new place brought a strange sense of hope, even if the effort of moving itself had worn us all out.

We were tired from the lifting, the packing, and the endless back-and-forth to get everything settled in the new house. But when we finally got there, it felt different. It felt like a new beginning.

I closed my eyes and let the warm water wash away the exhaustion of the day. The past had a way of creeping up on me, and it felt like memories from that time were coming back, slowly but surely.

The new house on Ashcresent was in a completely different neighborhood than the one we'd left behind. It felt strange at first, like we were in a completely different world. The area was quiet and unfamiliar, with houses that looked older and more spread out. It wasn't easy to get used to. But slowly, we started to find our rhythm. The house itself had its own charm — big rooms that felt empty at first, but with time, they started to fill with memories and laughter. I think that house became the backdrop for some of the most important years of my life, the ones that shaped who I was going to be.

I wasn't sure about a lot of things at that time, but I knew this house would become a part of me. There was something about the garage that was turned into a bedroom but was never insulated properly, creating a cold room no one wanted to sleep in; the sliding patio door, with its unique square bars, let in the sunlight and became the way we'd squeeze through when sneaking in and out of the house. The smell of dinner cooking from the kitchen made it feel like home. Even the neighborhood, though unfamiliar, started to grow on me. The huge backyard with the trail that led to the street became our gateway to the world outside — whether it was a shortcut to the corner store, a path to the park where we'd spend hours, or a way to explore other parts of the neighborhood without being seen.

But the biggest change came when it was time to start school again. I was about to enter 6th grade at Morningside Middle School, a place that felt like another new world I had to figure out. Morningside was on the Southside, right across from the Glen Garden Apartments. That school wasn't anything like the one I'd come from. The kids there were different, the teachers had their own way of running things, and the halls were full of faces I didn't recognize.

Making the transition was tough. At first, I felt like I didn't fit in. I had to learn how to find my place among new classmates and teachers. The school itself felt so different, too—there was a new kind of energy in the air, like everyone was in their own little world. But slowly, day by day, I started to get the hang of it. It wasn't easy, but it was something I had to do.

As the days passed, I started getting to know the neighborhood more, and something else happened that changed everything. I found out that Granny, Grama's sister, who lived just down the street, wasn't actually Grama's biological sister. At first, I didn't really understand what that meant. Granny had always been there for us, a constant presence in our lives. She wasn't blood, but that didn't matter. She was family in every way that mattered.

Granny was always a source of support for us, and her house felt like a safe haven. Since we didn't have a home telephone, she let us use hers whenever we needed to. We even gave her number to girls at school so they would think we had our own phone—it was embarrassing not having a phone.

Granny was generous in many ways. We would use her washing machine, which was a big help for us, and we loved wandering through her garden to pick fresh veggies. She had a special talent for taking care of animals, with her yard filled with pigeons and her playful dog named Muffin.

One of the things I cherished most about Granny was her sewing skills. I remember one time I needed some MC Hammer pants for a dance, and she whipped up a pair for me. They were amazing, and I felt so cool wearing them!

On weekends, Granny and Grama would throw parties filled with music and laughter. Those lively gatherings were always a blast. Granny's kindness and spirit inspired much of what I write in this book.

Granny (Left), Grama (Right)

One of the toughest things I had to deal with at Morningside was "6th grade jack-up day." It was a tradition where the older students would push around the younger ones. Kevin, my older brother, never had to go through it because no one dared to mess with him. By the time I made it to Morningside, I was nervous, but Kevin was so popular and had such a reputation that no one even thought about "jacking me up." His reputation alone kept me safe, and I never had to worry about being bullied that day. Kevin was always the type to handle things his own way, and his reputation spoke louder than any advice he could give me.

Kevin On Bike

That year, I was placed in Team Terrific. It was known for having unique teachers, and I quickly saw how different each of them was. Mrs. Hamilton, our English teacher, stood out. She was tough but fair. She didn't put up with anyone's nonsense, but she also had a sense of humor that made her classes interesting. I remember her teaching us the phrase "I beg your pardon." She explained it with so much detail, showing us how important it was to be polite and respectful when talking to others. That lesson stayed with me because it wasn't just about the words, but how we treated people.

Then there was Mrs. Dorothy, our Social Studies teacher. One day, I got into trouble with Joseph McGilvery during her class. We were messing around, and things got out of hand. We ended up in a fight, and because of that, I was moved to another class. That was a tough lesson for me. I learned that letting my emotions take over wasn't worth it, especially when it meant dealing with the consequences afterward.

Mrs. Campbell, our science teacher, was another big influence on me. She made learning so much fun.

She had a way of making biology come to life, helping me see how everything around us could be understood through science. I started to get really interested in how plants, animals, and even our own bodies worked. Her passion for science inspired me, and it became one of my favorite subjects.

Before Morningside, I had gone to Carroll Peak and Briscoe Elementary. It was at Briscoe where I had Miss. Brookins as my 5th grade teacher. She was tough but fair, and she really helped me build confidence in myself. I'll never forget how she pushed me to do better, even when I doubted myself. I still remember when Briscoe opened its doors for the first time. It was a big deal for all of us. I transitioned there, along with a lot of other students, and it felt like the beginning of a new chapter. It was exciting but also a little nerve-wracking because it was a new school with new teachers and classmates. That move, just like when we moved to the house on Ashcresent, felt like a fresh start, and it marked the start of a new phase in my school life.

As I adjusted to Morningside, it was clear that things were different from my previous schools. The halls were bigger, the students older, and the teachers more serious. But I also began to see how much I was learning and growing. I was figuring out how to balance schoolwork, friendships, and just trying to fit in. It wasn't always easy, but I felt proud of the progress I was making.

When I think back to my time at Carroll Peak and Briscoe, I realize how much those schools shaped who I was becoming. Briscoe wasn't small in terms of being a K-5 school, but it felt close-knit. I knew all the fifth graders and the teachers for fourth and fifth grades, which made it feel like a community. It was a place where I felt connected, surrounded by friends who felt like family.

But Morningside was different. It was bigger and more overwhelming, and suddenly, I felt lost in the crowd. It seemed like I didn't know anyone, and the busy hallways made it hard to feel at home. Even though I missed the tight-knit community of Briscoe, I knew that facing this new school was an important step in my life. I had to show myself that I could adapt and succeed, no matter how challenging it felt.

Looking back, some of the most vivid memories from those early days were the walks home from Carroll Peak with Kevin and Kasey. We were nervous about school, so one day we went to the bathroom to figure out what to do. After talking it over, we came up with a plan: we'd walk back home and tell Grama that we were sick. We thought it would work—until Grama showed us she wasn't having it. To our surprise, she drove us right back to school; her anger palpable in the car as we sat in silence. The tension was thick, and every passing second felt like an eternity. I could feel my heart pounding in my chest, knowing we were in deep trouble. I don't think I'd ever seen her that mad before.

None of us expected Grama to drive, but there she was, behind the wheel, taking us back when we thought we had gotten away with it. It was a wake-up call, and we quickly realized we couldn't pull one over on her.

But as much as we tested the limits with Grama, nothing prepared me for the real trouble I'd face at Briscoe. A kid named Lawrence. He was older, bigger, and he saw me as an easy target. Every day, he'd take my lunch money—just a few quarters, but at the time, it felt like everything. For a while, I let it happen. I didn't want to make waves and figured it was easier to just hand over the change than risk a fight.

That is, until Kevin caught wind of it.

Kevin used to go to the airport with our neighborhood cab driver, Big Fish, to make money. I had been asking for quarters, so eventually, he let me join them. Kevin had this whole system—he'd collect the luggage carts and return them for quarters. Although he was giving me an opportunity to make my own money, I just wanted to be with him. We'd race through the airport, sprinting for the carts, and he beat me every time. It didn't matter, though. I just liked tagging along.

Kevin came up with an idea, and at first, I thought he was joking. He said, "Why don't you go one way and I go another, and we'll meet back here at a certain time?" I was like, "Naw, man, we shouldn't split up." But Kevin, being Kevin, had his own plans. He tricked me. We got on this glass elevator, and just as the doors were closing, he jumped off, leaving me to head up alone. I was frantic. I could see him through the glass, pointing at his wrist like he was keeping time, but all I could think was that it was an accident and now I was lost. I just knew someone was going to kidnap me.

Looking for carts was the last thing on my mind. I wandered around, tears streaming down my face, until a security guard noticed me. "What's wrong with you?" he asked. I didn't want to say anything at first — two kids, about ten and twelve, alone at the airport with no parents in sight. But I couldn't hold it in. I burst into tears, telling him I was lost and that my brother had left me. I gave him a description, and they started checking the cameras. Sure enough, they spotted Kevin. They called out to him, and soon enough, he came around the corner. By that time, I was sitting in a chair, eating cookies, swinging my legs like nothing happened.

When I saw him, I was like, "You shouldn't have left me." He still doesn't let me live that down. But what I couldn't explain to him back then was that all I really wanted was to be with him. That kind of stuff was a no-go where I grew up. We didn't express feelings — not me, especially. I was already a target for being different. So I kept it all inside, even then.

After Kevin found out about me being bullied, he was furious. He waited until Lawrence got off the bus, and then he took matters into his own hands. They fought, and Kevin made it clear—after he had pretty much beaten him up—that Lawrence needed to leave me alone. From that day on, Lawrence stayed away. Kevin didn't say much, but his actions spoke louder than words ever could.

In that moment, I realized that Kevin was always looking out for me, even if he had a funny way of showing it.

It wasn't just about lunch money anymore—it was about dignity. And I'd learned how to protect mine.

Ashcresent was also where my interest in medicine first sparked. Momma was studying to become a nurse's aide at the time, and I'd help her study. She had this incredible imagination and would set up our rooms like hospitals, getting all the kids in the neighborhood and our cousins to play along. I was always the doctor. While other kids were asking for toy guns and handcuffs for Christmas, I was the one asking for a "doctor's kit"—and they all laughed at me for it.

One day, while I was at the hospital with Grama, I overheard a doctor talking to his patient. He asked, "What color are your stools?"—one of the vocabulary words I'd just helped Momma study the day before. My face lit up, and I whispered, "I know what that means." That moment stuck with me. From then on, I grabbed hold of the idea of studying medicine.

Ashcrescent is also when my Uncle Michael first went to jail. Uncle Michael was the only male figure that kept us in line. He was the disciplinarian—though his methods would be considered child abuse today, back then, he was the one keeping us in line and making us tough. Unfortunately, he was also addicted to crack cocaine. He'd come home on Fridays after getting paid, slip me $10 or $20, and tell me to cover for him—to tell his baby momma that he was nowhere to be found. By the time Sunday came around, he had smoked up his whole check, and if I hadn't spent that $10 or $20, he'd come back asking for it.

One day, the police caught him buying some crack. He went to jail, and it was devastating for us to see him in handcuffs. Things seemed to go downhill from there. The worst part was how the system just didn't get it—how crucial it was to have a Black man in the home, raising young Black boys like us. They removed him for something he really needed rehab for, not prison time. It was like they didn't see the ripple effect it would have—how pulling him out of our lives made statistics out of my brothers and could've done the same to me.

Instead of seeing a man struggling with addiction and offering help, they saw another number to process. But for us, he was more than that. Losing him to the system left a void that the streets would fill.

Thinking back, it's kind of wild that a place like Ashcresent, with all the chaos and trouble, was also where I first started dreaming about a better future.

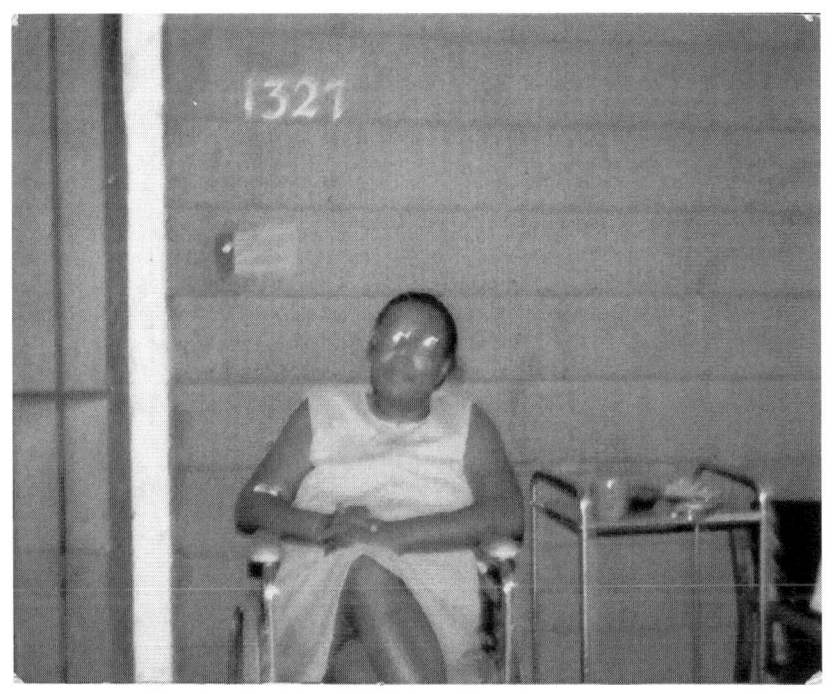

Grama at 1327 Stewart St

Chapter Seven

Choices and Consequences

You've made a choice, but it might cost you everything.

Growing up with Kevin and Kasey was an intense experience. Both of them were naturally tough and well-liked by everyone. They had this commanding presence that made people respect them without question. It felt like they were the ones everyone turned to, and, whether I liked it or not, that had a huge impact on how I navigated the world around me. They were the ones setting the example for how we were supposed to act, and their way of doing things became the standard that I subconsciously measured myself against.

Kevin, in particular, was always the protector. He had this strong, no-nonsense attitude that made people think twice before they even thought about messing with me. Whenever there was a situation where I was in trouble, Kevin was there in an instant, ready to step in and handle things. It gave me this incredible sense of security—knowing that no matter what happened, I always had Kevin to back me up.

One time, when we were staying at the Ambassador's apartments, I learned just how much I depended on him. I was about thirteen years old, and there was this huge guy—had to be at least 6'3" and 300 pounds—who usually dressed as a woman. He did something that felt too playful, too suspicious for my liking. I can't remember exactly what it was—maybe he squirted me with a water gun—but I didn't like it one bit. Without thinking, I grabbed a two-by-four and smacked him across the face. The wood snapped in half, but it didn't stop him. His eyes turned red with anger, and he came after me. I took off running, heart pounding, not sure if my brother and his friends had already left. When I turned the corner and saw Kevin standing there, a wave of relief washed over me. My whole expression changed because I knew, without a doubt, that with Kevin there, everything was going to be okay. I didn't have to worry about a thing—that was the kind of protector he was.

But as much as I appreciated having that safety net, it also planted a belief in my mind. I started to feel like I needed to be tough too. If I was going to keep up with my brothers and earn the respect of those around me, I couldn't be the "weak" one. I had to learn how to defend myself, stand my ground, and hold my own. I realized that while Kevin's protection was great, there would be times when I couldn't rely on him to fix things for me.

I didn't have to fight often because Kevin and Kasey took care of the older kids, while Brandon and Leisa handled the younger ones. But there was this one time when Brandon got into it with a kid who was too old for him but too young for Kevin and Kasey. So, sure enough, they came to get me. I was at home, minding my own business, when they rushed in and told me to put on some shoes—I had to go fight this dude. I was like, "Okay," figuring it was my turn to return the favor.

The kid was waiting in the field around the corner from our house. I didn't have anything against him, but I knew I had to fight. I walked up and said, "Man, I gotta fight you," but before I could get anything else out, he hauled off and punched me right in the face. To this day, I never let anyone get the first lick. We started fighting immediately. He tried to scoop me, but I was ready—fighting and wrestling were all we did at home. He couldn't get me on the ground, and I was punching his head like it was a punching bag.

Somehow, we ended up on the ground anyway, with me on top, swinging. He was scooting back, trying to get away, and then blood started coming from somewhere. I felt it as I kept swinging—punch,

punch—blood splashing like water. I could hear him screaming, and I remember thinking, there's no way I'm hitting him that hard. Then I looked down and realized he had rolled onto a broken beer bottle, slicing his thigh open deep.

I stopped immediately, reaching out to help him up, but my brother grabbed me, scolding me for trying to help. They still give me grief about that to this day. I hoped the kid was okay, honestly.

A while later, I was walking home when his big brother jumped out of a car, ready to beat me up, claiming we had jumped his little brother.

It wasn't just about being physically strong; it was also about building up the inner strength to face challenges on my own. Over time, I came to understand that true strength meant being able to handle things independently, even when I felt like I was in over my head. Kevin taught me that, in his own way, but it was up to me to take that lesson and apply it to my own life.

Kasey, on the other hand, was more rebellious. He was always challenging the rules, pushing boundaries, and never seemed afraid to stand out. His boldness was something I couldn't help but admire. While Kevin was the protector, Kasey was the one who lived by his own rules, and he didn't care who disagreed with him. He had a way of walking into any situation, acting like he owned it, and never backing down from anyone. It was like he had this confidence that made him untouchable, and honestly, I was drawn to it.

It was Kasey who first introduced me to the idea of "acting tough." He showed me that sometimes, in order to fit in or avoid trouble, you had to put on a tough exterior, even if it didn't always align with who you really were inside. I started adopting that mentality, especially when I was with him. When we were together, it felt like the world was ours for the taking, and if anyone challenged us, they'd have to deal with the consequences. It wasn't always easy to maintain, though. There were times when I would act tough just to keep up with Kasey, even if it wasn't really how I felt on the inside. But I learned that sometimes, pretending to be something you're not is just a way to survive in certain situations.

One day, I remember walking with Kasey and Kevin outside of school. We were lined up in a row, walking down the sidewalk like we owned it. We had this unspoken rule—if anyone bumped into us or challenged us in any way, it was a guaranteed fight. It was the kind of challenge that Kasey seemed to thrive on. He wasn't scared of anything, and he made sure we weren't either. That day, we dared anyone to make a move. If they did, there was no backing down. But even though I went along with it, a part of me was uneasy. It was one thing to act tough and walk with confidence, but it was another to be ready for what might happen next.

That experience, however, taught me something important: how to stay composed, even when everything around you is escalating. In the face of confrontation, I learned how to hold my ground, even if I wasn't always sure of myself. It was like a test of my own inner strength. Kasey's boldness and willingness to face challenges head-on made me realize that sometimes, staying calm in the middle of chaos was a strength in itself. But even though I got through that moment, it made me realize that there was a fine line between acting tough and actually being tough. And sometimes, that line was hard to see.

My mother had her struggles, particularly with crack cocaine, which made it difficult for her to always be the kind of parent we needed. Despite this, there was one thing that never wavered—her faith in God. No matter what she was going through, her spirituality remained a constant in our lives. Although she bounced around from church to church, even during the hardest times, my mom always encouraged us to stay close to God. She believed that faith could guide us through the toughest challenges, and she often reminded us that no matter what happened, God would always be there for us. One of the most memorable churches was Concord Missionary Baptist Church. They'd send a van out to pick us up for services, and one day when the driver, a kind man named Mr. Lawrence, asked why I hadn't been attending, I told him it was because I didn't have any dress shoes. Without hesitation, he drove us to a local, inexpensive shoe store, Payless, which eventually closed down after places like Wal-Mart came to town. He bought me my very first pair of dress shoes — pointed toes with little tassels dangling on the front. I was so excited about those shoes. They felt like more than just footwear; they were a sign that someone cared enough to help me get to church, and they became a symbol of that support.

But there was a side to my mother's struggles that I didn't fully understand at the time. She often carried a sense of guilt, believing that our mistakes or missteps were somehow her fault. She thought that her own challenges as a parent, particularly the way she struggled with addiction, reflected poorly on us as her children.

My mom believed wholeheartedly in the spiritual saying that a mother bears the weight of her children's sins. She carried this burden until we turned thirteen, believing that every wrong turn we made was a reflection of her own shortcomings. It created a heavy atmosphere at home, one where her guilt hung over us constantly—a reminder that every mistake we made wasn't just ours to bear but hers too.

But as I grew older, I began to understand something important—that her struggles were not a reflection of her love for us. They were part of her own journey, just as our challenges were a part of ours. It wasn't her fault. Life was complicated, and sometimes people had to face their battles in different ways. Her love for us was never in question, even when her actions didn't always align with the care we needed.

As Kevin and Kasey got older, their paths started to diverge; they became more involved with dangerous groups, and places like Prince Hall and Pilgrim Valley Apartments seemed to become regular stops for them. Losing Uncle Michael to the system made Kevin and Kasey more unpredictable. They didn't lose faith in what we'd grown up on; they just didn't have a man around to raise them—only women. It was a world I couldn't fully understand, but I could see how the absence of a strong male figure left them searching for direction in all the wrong places. They started drifting—not from faith, or respect, but from the guidance that had once enforced those things. Without Uncle Michael, their choices became bolder and riskier, like they were testing the limits just to feel something solid beneath their feet. It was hard to watch, knowing that the streets were quick to fill the void he left behind. I wanted to hold on to the values we were raised with, but I also knew that without the right guidance, even the best intentions can go astray.

I, on the other hand, made a promise to myself that I wouldn't follow in Kevin and Kasey's footsteps. I chose a different path—one that didn't lead to the chaos and danger they were getting involved with. I stayed at home more, keeping my distance from the trouble they were finding. It was hard to watch them test their limits, especially when it felt like they were heading down a road I didn't want to go down. Their behavior created a lot of tension between us. They couldn't understand why I wasn't joining them, and I didn't always understand why they were making the choices they were. But in a way, their actions pushed me even harder to find my own way, to figure out who I wanted to be and how I could live a life that was different from theirs.

Choosing to stay home more often came with its own challenges. It led to a sense of isolation because I wasn't as involved socially as the other kids my age. I often found myself on the outside looking in. But over time, I came to see that this isolation wasn't entirely a bad thing. It gave me the space I needed to reflect on my own choices and think about who I was becoming. It helped me realize that I didn't have to be defined by the actions of my brothers or anyone else. I could create my own identity, separate from the chaos around me.

I began to feel like the black sheep, as everyone around me was doing things that kids our age shouldn't have been doing. When you really look at it, though, I was doing what normal kids should be doing—being home before dark, not roaming the streets at twelve or thirteen, robbing or trying to sell drugs. But where I grew up, that was the norm. What I was doing—just being a kid—was actually abnormal to them. It made me stand out even more, but in a way, it helped me realize that I had to forge my own path, no matter how different it seemed to those around me.

Looking back, I wasn't always aware of it at the time, but my faith in God became a quiet source of strength. It helped me navigate the turbulence that was swirling around me—at home, with my brothers, and in the world in general. When things felt overwhelming, when I didn't know what to do or where to turn, my belief in something greater than myself kept me steady. Even if I didn't have all the answers, I knew that God was there, offering me the strength I needed to keep moving. Growing up in Morningside, Briscoe, and Ashcresent taught me valuable lessons about resilience. The challenges we faced as a family became a crucible—testing us, pushing us to our limits, and ultimately shaping who I was becoming. It wasn't always easy, but those struggles had a purpose. They helped me understand what it really meant to survive, to fight through the hard times, and to grow from them.

Through the ups and downs, I learned the importance of family—not just in a physical sense, but also in the emotional support and connections we share. My brothers, with all their struggles and moments of strength, showed me the complexities of life. They taught me how to navigate the fine line between right and wrong, and what it meant to stand by the people you love, even when they made choices that didn't always align with your values. Teachers like Miss. Brookins and Mrs. Hamilton showed me that learning wasn't just about textbooks and tests, but also about understanding who you are and how you can contribute to the world around you. They instilled in me a sense of self-belief and the importance of perseverance, even when life wasn't fair. They encouraged me to keep pushing forward, to always express myself, and to value education, not just as a means to an end, but as a tool to understand and shape the world.

In addition to the lessons learned at school, the family dynamic played a huge role. I saw firsthand the power of determination through the struggles and triumphs of my brothers. Kevin and Kasey, with all their boldness and rebellion, taught me the hard costs of poor choices. I witnessed how one misstep could lead to consequences that couldn't easily be undone. Yet, I also saw their strength and their resilience—how they kept fighting, kept pushing, and kept trying to find their way. That was a powerful lesson. It wasn't about being perfect—it was about never giving up, no matter how hard things got.

Chapter Eight

The First Gun Shot

The bullet doesn't care who you are or what you've done—it just knows where to land.

The tension in the room was thick, and it felt like the air was heavy with what had just happened. Kevin held the shotgun shell in his hand, not seeming to care about the danger. He didn't seem to understand it—or maybe he just didn't care. Then, with a quick motion, he pushed the bolt forward hard enough to make me flinch, and I had no idea what would happen next.

And then—BANG!

The noise hit me like a slap to the face. It was so loud that it shook me to my bones. The chair I was sitting in jerked back, spinning a little as pieces of wood and orange splinters flew in front of me, hanging in the air for a split second before falling. My ears were ringing, and everything around me blurred. For a moment, I couldn't understand what had just happened.

I sat there, frozen, confused. Had I been shot? My mind was racing, trying to piece everything together, but all I could hear was the ringing in my ears. Slowly, I started to realize what had happened. My eyes shot to Kevin. His face was pale, and his eyes were wide with fear. But that didn't make me feel better—not at all.

"Did you shoot me? Did you shoot me?" I yelled, panic filling my chest, making it hard to breathe.

Kevin's voice was calm, almost too calm. "Nah, boy, shut up." He waved off my fear, like it was nothing. But the terror inside me didn't go away. His words didn't make my head stop pounding or make the cold sweat stop creeping down my back.

I looked at the chair where my arm had been just seconds ago. There was a hole in the backrest, big and jagged, and the bullet had gone right through where my arm had been. It had gone through the chair and into the wall behind me. My heart was pounding in my chest. I realized that I had barely avoided being shot, maybe even killed.

Kevin looked at the hole, his eyes a little nervous, but he still didn't seem to get how serious this was. Fear filled the air between us, heavy and thick. My brain was trying to catch up, trying to understand what had just happened.

"We were just hammering," I said quickly, the words rushing out before I could stop them. The neighbor didn't look convinced, but he didn't push it any further. He just nodded, mumbling something under his breath, and walked back to his house. He wasn't fully buying it, but he decided to let it go. We had gotten away with it—this time.

Kevin and I wasted no time. We ran across the street to my momma's house. My stomach was tied in knots with every step. As soon as we got inside, I couldn't hold it in anymore. The words spilled out as I collapsed into a chair, my voice trembling with guilt. "I'm sorry," I kept saying, over and over, like somehow my apologies could fix everything. Momma didn't seem to notice how desperate I was. But when we told her what had happened—how we covered it up and what could've happened—she snapped into action. Her calmness was like a mask, but it was so practiced. I watched her try to cover the hole in the wall with a certificate. It was ridiculous, trying to hide the damage with something that couldn't possibly make sense. The hole was at waist height, way too obvious for a certificate to work. But she acted like it was the perfect solution. I couldn't help but let out a bitter laugh. It was absurd, but somehow it worked. Grama never questioned it, though she didn't talk to

Kevin about it either. Later, I would find out it was Momma who took the blame.

I stood up, my legs shaky, and slowly walked toward Kevin, still in shock. "What if I had been shot?" I asked, barely able to speak.

But Kevin didn't answer. He just stared at me, his fear hidden behind his tough act that I wasn't sure I could trust.

But the guilt didn't stop there.

It wasn't just about the gunshot. It wasn't just about the hole in the wall. It was about everything that had led me to this point—everything that had built up over time. There were moments when I truly felt like my mother hated me, moments when I wondered if I even mattered to her.

I had tried so hard to show her that I cared. When I earned a little money cutting the grass one summer, I bought her two angel statues. I thought they were beautiful, something she could keep in the house, a symbol of love and respect. I gave them to her with hope in my heart, hoping she would appreciate them, hoping she would see the effort I had put into making her happy.

But when we had another argument—one of the many—it felt like everything I had done for her meant nothing. She grabbed the angels, tossed them out the door, and shattered them on the pavement. I remember standing there, watching the fragile pieces of what I had given her lying in pieces on the ground. My heart shattered right along with them. I stood there, numb, trying to understand how someone who was supposed to love me could do something like that.

And then there was the incident with my red jeans—the ones that looked like Jabot pants, the ones I had been so proud of. They were my best pair, the ones that made me feel cool, that made me feel like I belonged. But it didn't matter to her. She was angry again, and in her rage, she cut them up. The familiar feeling of devastation washed over me. They weren't just pants—they were a part of me, something that gave me a sense of self, and she had destroyed them without a second thought.

The neglect, the anger, the feeling of being unseen—each moment added weight to the burden I carried. And I didn't know how to shake it off. I didn't know how to make it stop.

In retaliation, I found myself reaching for the nearest tool of destruction—my mother's dresses. She never treated me with the love I thought I deserved, and I wanted to make her feel just a fraction of the hurt I had been carrying. I took a clothes hanger and ripped up her dresses while she wasn't home. I wanted her to know what it felt like to lose something you cared about, to feel the sting of betrayal.

Months later, when she discovered the holes in her dresses, she immediately knew it was me. The connection was too obvious, too raw. The realization hit me like a punch to the gut. She had finally found out. I hadn't been able to escape her wrath, and now the consequences were inevitable.

But none of that seemed to matter anymore.

I had reached a point where the pain became too much to carry, and I began to think about ending it all. The weight of everything—my fractured relationship with my mom, the constant sense of being alone—pushed me to the brink. I remember standing in front of the flower bed in our living room, feeling the hopelessness wash over me. The white bricks of the flower bed, which once seemed so harmless, became my only focus. I tied a shoelace around my neck and looped it over the hook, planning to end it, to escape the pain that felt unending.

But in the end, I couldn't even escape that. The hook broke as I jumped, and the shoelace tightened around my neck, choking me. I thought I was going to die there, in that room, with nothing but the silence of my own thoughts to accompany me.

The air around my neck seemed to vanish as the shoelace tightened. My hands shot up instinctively, but they couldn't escape the pressure. My throat constricted, each breath growing more difficult to take. I could feel my face turning red, panic rising as I struggled against the growing weight of my own body, teetering on the edge of consciousness.

I fought, desperate to breathe, but there was nothing to hold on to, nothing to break the cycle. My vision blurred, and my hands felt numb as they scraped against the brick, desperate for something solid to grip. The world started to tilt, a sense of darkness creeping in, and it felt like I was suffocating from the inside out.

In that moment, I thought it was over. I thought this was the end.

But my mother was in the kitchen, she watched me—watched me choke—but she didn't intervene. She didn't come rushing to cut the lace, didn't try to stop me from ending it. It was Kevin who finally saved me, rushing over with a sense of urgency, his hands shaking as he cut through the lace with a steak knife. I gasped for air as the tension around my neck was released. I crumpled to the floor, dizzy and gasping, but still alive. Kevin didn't say a word, but his eyes were wide with a fear I hadn't seen before.

I never spoke about it to anyone. Not Kevin, not my mom. But I wondered, deep down, why my mother hadn't come to my aid. Why she had watched me struggle.

The scars, though, weren't just physical.

There was another moment when my mother left a permanent mark on me, not just on my body but on my soul. It happened during one of our many arguments—those bitter exchanges that always ended in more pain than resolution. This time, it was an ink pen.

She had always been quick to anger, quick to lash out when she was upset, and this time, I happened to be in the wrong place at the wrong time. The pen jabbed into my stomach—hard. The pain was sharp, like a burn, and I could feel the tip digging into my skin, leaving a mark that would stay with me long after the anger had faded.

I looked down, barely able to comprehend what had just happened. A deep, dark scar formed where the pen had struck, and for a moment, I thought it looked like an appendix scar. It seemed fitting in a way—like the wound had been carved into me, marking me for something deeper than just pain. It was a reminder of how my mother's anger had torn through me, physically and emotionally. The scar was there to remind me of how little I mattered in the face of her rage.

To this day, that scar never fully healed. Neither did I.

One day, Kevin and I were outside when we noticed a man visiting our mom, who was parking his car crookedly. It seemed like a minor mistake, but Kevin, true to his nature, couldn't help but point it out to the driver. "You parked crooked," Kevin said casually.

The man, clearly irritated, tossed the keys to Kevin without a second thought, as though handing over control of the car was no big deal. "Fix it," he said, his voice almost bored.

At that moment, I watched in disbelief as Kevin—at just thirteen—jumped into the driver's seat, tossing the keys around in his hands with the same ease he handled everything else in his life. I climbed into the passenger seat, unsure of what to think. We didn't have much gas, just $2 worth, but that didn't stop Kevin. He started the car and pulled out onto the street, the sound of the engine humming under the tension in the air.

We drove around aimlessly, the world feeling bigger and more exciting with every turn. But then, as we cruised down the street, I noticed the same man running toward the car, his face red with anger. He was shouting, demanding the keys back. It took me a moment to realize what had happened—the man hadn't given Kevin permission to drive. He had just tossed him the keys out of frustration, expecting someone to fix the problem, but Kevin had misread the situation.

The man's anger boiled over, and I could see his eyes filled with fury as he demanded the keys. Kevin, always quick on his feet, sped away before the man could catch up, but it didn't stop the situation from escalating.

When we got back, we didn't hear from the man again. He never returned to see my mom, and I was left wondering what had happened—why he'd given Kevin the keys in the first place. Kevin never fully explained it to me, and I never asked. The mystery of it lingered, a part of Kevin's life that I didn't quite understand.

But that night, the consequences came. Uncle Michael found out. And he wasn't pleased.

Uncle Mike didn't mince words. He whooped us, his fury aimed squarely at Kevin. He was the one who had made the decision, who had misread the situation, and it was Kevin who faced the brunt of Uncle Michael's anger. I begged and pleaded, insisting that I had been just following Kevin, but it didn't matter. Kevin was the older one, and he bore the full weight of the punishment.

It was a lesson I wouldn't forget. Kevin wasn't always unbeatable. He wasn't always the one who got away with everything. In that moment, I saw the weakness behind his tough exterior, and I began to understand that life wasn't as easy as he made it seem.

Chapter Nine

A False Role Model

What seems perfect on the outside might be troubled within.

It was a sunny afternoon when we first met Bruce. He wasn't really related to us, but we called him Uncle Bruce anyway. Bruce was one of the few younger Black men we knew who had money. He drove a shiny car and lived on the East Side, in Woodhaven. At the time, it seemed like he had everything—a nice house, money, and a car that made him stand out. We were all impressed, especially me.

I was just a kid, and like a lot of kids, I looked up to people who seemed successful. Bruce looked like someone who had it all figured out, and I thought maybe he could show us the way out of our struggles. He didn't spend much time with me, but when he did, I could tell that he thought he was better than the rest of us. Still, I admired him because, to me, he was the example of what I thought I wanted to be one day.

Even though he seemed like a role model, I didn't really get to spend much time with him. He was always busy with the older kids. But whenever he came around, he had stories to tell, about places he'd been, things he'd done. He had this way of talking that made everything sound so exciting. I wanted to be like him, but I didn't know much about him beyond the surface.

As time passed, I started to see things a little clearer. I began to realize that Bruce wasn't the man I had imagined. He wasn't the perfect role model I thought he was. I started noticing the way he treated people, especially the ones he didn't care about. He had money, but it didn't make him any better than anyone else.

As I navigated the tricky waters of middle school, I found myself searching for someone to look up to, hoping to find a role model. Bruce was that person—at least, I thought he was. He had a way of drawing people in with his charm, and many admired him. But beneath that confident surface, there was more than met the eye.

One day, I faced a challenge that felt huge to me. My eighth-grade graduation was coming up, and the dress code was clear: I needed a white button-down shirt, black pants, and black shoes. I didn't own a white dress shirt, so I decided to ask Bruce for help, thinking he would understand. After all, he had the money to help.

But when I asked him if he could help me get the shirt, his answer shocked me. "No," he said, waving his hand as if my request was a bother. In that moment, I felt a wave of confusion and disappointment wash over me. How could someone I admired turn me down so easily? His reaction wasn't the kind of support I expected from a role model. Instead of helping, he made it clear that he was more interested in showing off than actually helping anyone.

Looking back, I see that Bruce was more focused on his own image than on teaching important lessons about kindness and generosity. He showed me that sometimes the people we look up to don't always have our best interests at heart. What I really needed was someone who would help me and teach me the value of caring for others.

As I stood there, watching my classmates walk from the classroom to the gym for graduation, I felt a wave of disappointment wash over me. In that moment, I learned a tough lesson about trust. True role models don't just enjoy the spotlight; they help others and offer support without expecting anything in return. Bruce's refusal to help me became an important lesson about trust that I would remember long after this day.

One day, a group of us was walking to the store when we saw a man standing by the side of the road. His car was stalled, and he looked like he was having trouble. He was a skinny white guy with glasses, and when he saw us, he asked if one of us could help him.

He needed someone with "little fingers" to help him pull out a fuse, and one of my brothers volunteered. The man was grateful, and after my brother helped him, he offered him money. He also said that he might have a job for my brother in the future. He took the money, and just like that, the man said he needed to take my brother with him for a bit.

At first, it didn't seem strange. All my brothers often stayed out late, and we didn't think much of it.

But as the hours went by, we started to wonder where he was. By the time it got dark, I was getting worried. I told Grama, and she decided to call the police.

When the police arrived, we hadn't heard from my brother yet. We were all on edge, waiting for him to come home. Then, just as the police were starting to ask questions, the man, Steve, pulled up with my brother. He looked fine. The man didn't seem worried or scared at all. He acted like nothing had happened.

The police were confused. There wasn't much they could do. Steve hadn't done anything illegal, as far as they could tell. He just dropped my brother off like it was a normal thing. The authorities didn't press charges, and Steve drove away, leaving us with more questions than answers.

I couldn't shake the feeling that something was wrong. My brother had been with a stranger all day, and no one seemed to care. There was no apology from

Steve, no sign that he understood how messed up it was to take someone's kid and just drive off with them. But my brother was back, so we tried to move on. But for me, that moment stuck with me. It was a lesson about how little control we had over our own lives.

Life at Ashcresent wasn't easy. Money was always tight. We were constantly struggling to pay the bills, and it was becoming harder to keep up with basic things like electricity and water. I remember when the electric bill went unpaid for a few months, and the lights were cut off. We made do by using candles, and I would always hear my momma and Grama talking about how we were going to get by. We couldn't use too much water because the water bill was also overdue and was eventually turned off too. Chatney was always good at gaming the system; he would reconnect the lights from the house meter and turn on the water from the street; we would fill up tubs and buckets, and then shut it off before the meter reader came. It felt like a game, but the fear of being caught was always there.

Eventually, the electric company came and cut the power from the pole altogether. My grandmother had already used up all the names she could to get the utilities in our name. She had used her name, my mom's, and even both of my uncles' names just to get the lights and water back on. It was getting to the point where we couldn't even rely on those tricks anymore.

That's when we decided to move. We needed to find a place with all bills paid, and that's when we ended up moving from the South Side of Fort Worth to an apartment complex called The Meadows on the East Side. This was a huge change for us, especially since the East Side was known as Blood territory, while we had always lived in Crip territory on the South Side. Kevin, in particular, struggled with this shift. He had to move out because he couldn't stay around the Bloods any longer. Finding a place with all bills paid led us to this new apartment, but it felt like we were stepping into a completely different world. As we settled in, I could see that Kevin wasn't adjusting well. Things seemed to be getting worse for him; it felt like everything was falling apart. He didn't fit in like he used to, and I could see the struggle in his eyes. Watching him go through this was hard, especially since we used to be so close.

Just as we were packing up to leave Ashcresent, Steve showed up again. The same guy who had taken my brother with him all that time ago. At first, we weren't sure what to make of it, but Steve offered to help us move. Grama and Momma didn't hesitate to accept his offer. Moving from Ashcresent to the East Side was going to be a big job, and we didn't have the resources to do it ourselves.

Steve kept his word, although he was a bit late. He showed up with a U-Haul truck, ready to help us load everything up. I don't know what it was, but I felt uneasy around him. Even though my brother had returned safely, I couldn't shake the feeling that something wasn't right with Steve. But he helped us move, and at least for that day, he wasn't causing any trouble.

As we were packing up, Steve started asking me questions. One of the first things he asked was if I had ever been to Six Flags. I told him I hadn't, and that's when I remembered my real dad, Randolph Dawkins. I had been so excited when I was younger because he promised to take me to Six Flags when he got out of jail. He wrote me a letter saying he would, but I waited all day on the porch for him to show up, and he never did. I was just a kid back then, but the disappointment cut deep. I didn't want to admit it, but I felt stupid for even thinking he would keep that promise.

But when Steve brought up Six Flags again, I felt a spark of hope. Maybe this time, things would be different. Maybe this man, who had helped us out, would be the one to take me somewhere exciting. But then, he said I couldn't tell anyone. He wanted it to be a surprise, just between him and me. I wasn't sure how to feel, but it was hard not to be a little excited. I still felt like maybe, just maybe, this time would be different. Steve promised he would take us all, but he asked me to keep it a secret. It was strange, but I didn't think too much of it at the time.

As the day went on and we continued packing, Steve's offer lingered in my mind. At only twelve, I couldn't help but feel a spark of hope. After all, this was a chance to do something special—something I had been dreaming about for a long time. Six Flags was more than just a theme park to me; it represented something much bigger. It was a promise that had been broken before, but maybe this time, Steve could help make it a reality.

Even though I still felt a little uneasy about him, I pushed those feelings aside. Maybe I was just being paranoid. Maybe Steve wasn't the same man he had been when he first took my brother away. He seemed like a nice guy now, offering to take all of us on a fun trip. He kept saying it would be a surprise, and I told myself it would be just that—a surprise for everyone.

I kept thinking about Six Flags, and I realized I was ready for a break from all the stress we had been living with. Moving to the East Side had been tough, and Kevin's struggles made everything harder. Maybe a day of fun was exactly what we needed. I tried to put aside all the bad things that had happened and let myself believe in the possibility of something good. After all, it was just a trip to an amusement park, right? It couldn't hurt.

As we continued to pack, Steve was still hanging around, helping us load things up and chatting with us. At first, I tried to ignore the discomfort in my stomach. But then, something happened that made me more uneasy.

I had been carrying boxes all day, and by the time we were almost done, my back started to ache. It wasn't anything new. I had always had back problems, and Grama used to joke that I didn't have a back, just "gristle" or something. But this time, when I told Steve about my sore back, he offered to "pop" it for me.

Now, that wasn't anything unusual, really. People would do that sometimes, you know? They would grab you and twist your arms around to relieve the tension. But there was something off about Steve's offer. He didn't just casually mention it—he insisted. I told him I was fine, that I didn't need help. But he wasn't listening. He kept saying, "It'll make you feel better."

I didn't want to make a big deal out of it, so I agreed. He crossed my arms in front of me, and then he stepped behind me. It wasn't like how it normally went when someone would just lightly twist your body to ease the pain. He grabbed me too tightly, and I could feel the pressure as he tried to force my body into a position I didn't want to be in. I told him I was good again, but he didn't stop right away.

Finally, I pulled away and said, "Nah, I'm good." That was enough to get him to stop, but my heart was racing. Something didn't feel right about the whole thing. I told myself it was nothing, that maybe I was just overreacting. But deep down, the feeling was growing—something about Steve just didn't sit right with me.

Even though I tried to brush off the situation, the unease kept gnawing at me. Steve had been nice enough, but I couldn't ignore the feeling that something was wrong. He wasn't like the other people who had helped us over the years. He wasn't like Bruce, who had his own kind of charm but had his own issues too. Bruce wasn't perfect, but Steve... Steve seemed different. There was something darker about him that I couldn't put into words.

Still, I tried to push the thought away. I mean, he was just helping us move, right? And he promised he would take us to Six Flags, something that seemed like it could be a nice, fun escape from everything. It wasn't like we had many options for fun, and I told myself that maybe I was just being too cautious. After all, things hadn't gotten worse yet, right?

But the more I thought about it, the more I started to realize that something didn't add up. Why was he so insistent on keeping things a secret? Why did he feel the need to be so involved in our lives, especially when we didn't know much about him? And most importantly, why did he insist on touching me the way he did?

As we finished moving, I couldn't shake the feeling that I had made a mistake. The whole time we were loading up, I had felt like something was off, like I was being too trusting. I wanted to tell someone, but who could I tell? My mom? Grama? They would've just brushed it off, I was sure of it. They probably wouldn't even understand what I was feeling.

So, we all piled into the car—me, Kevin, Kasey, and Steve. I kept my mouth shut about the whole Six

Flags plan. I had promised Steve I wouldn't tell anyone, and I didn't want to mess that up. But even then, something about being alone with Steve felt wrong.

He drove us to Prince Hall, and I could see Kevin and Kasey getting out of the car. They didn't seem too concerned, but I noticed that I was the only one left in the car with Steve.

"That's okay," Steve said with a grin. "I guess they didn't want to go. It's just me and you now."

I wasn't sure how to react. Kevin and Kasey both seemed uncomfortable too, but I figured if they didn't think much of it then I would be alright. I had been through worse, right?

But as we drove on, I started feeling more and more uncomfortable. Steve was asking me a bunch of questions—nothing serious, just random things—but I could tell he was trying to get under my skin. It was like he was testing me, seeing how much he could get away with.

When we stopped at a Burger King drive-thru, I started to wonder what exactly was going to happen next.

The next part was when I started to get really uneasy. Steve told me he had an "awesome idea." He wanted me to drive. I didn't think too much about it at first. It sounded fun, and I was just a kid, so I figured it would be cool to try. But when I got into the front seat, I realized the only way I could reach the wheel was by sitting in Steve's lap. It felt strange, but I didn't say anything at first.

We started driving through the woods, and then, out of nowhere, Steve made a weird comment about Michael Jackson. You know, how Michael would grab his crotch when he danced. He said something like, "You're like Michael Jackson, huh?" And when he said it, his hands were all over me.

That's when it clicked. I realized what was happening. I was terrified. This was not the trip I had thought it would be. This wasn't a fun day at Six Flags. It was something much worse.

I jumped out of his lap, my heart pounding, and told him to take me home. But Steve didn't take it well. His expression darkened, and he acted like I had insulted him. "I'm just testing you to see if you're safe to come to my house," he said, his voice eerily calm.

I knew better. Something was wrong.

When I insisted again, his response sent a chill down my spine. He told me he wasn't taking me home. Instead, he threatened to leave me in the woods, alone. Panic surged through me. I felt trapped. I wanted to scream, but I couldn't. In that moment, I had no choice but to agree to go with him.

All I wanted was to get out of there. I just wanted to go home.

By the time we arrived at his house, I was a wreck. My stomach was twisted in knots, and I felt sick to my core. Steve had a wife and a baby boy, and for a moment, I thought maybe I would be safe there. But when I went to change, Steve walked right into the room, and I had to hurry and wrap a towel around me. He said, "Man, nobody wants to see you," but it felt like he was trying to intimidate me.

After the night at his house, things just felt... off. We went to Six Flags the next day, but I didn't have fun. I kept thinking about what had happened, and I just wanted to go home.

When we finally got back to the new apartment, I didn't say a word. I just ran inside and collapsed in the bathroom, not even needing to use it. I cried. I was scared, confused, and ashamed. How could I have been so naive?

I didn't tell anyone about what had happened. Not Grama, not my mom, not even Kevin. I couldn't.

And that's when I knew. I had no idea what Steve's true intentions were, but I was sure of one thing: I couldn't trust him. Not anymore.

To anyone reading this story, I want to emphasize that as a child, it is never your fault if someone takes advantage of you. You are not to blame for the actions of others, no matter how confusing or frightening the situation may feel. It's important to remember that you should never keep secrets from your parents or trusted adults.

The devil wants you to feel alone, as if you have no one to talk to, but I assure you, you are not alone. There are people who care and want to help you. If you find yourself in a situation where you feel uncomfortable or scared, reach out to someone you trust—whether it's a parent, a teacher, or a friend.

Parents, please be vigilant and mindful about who you leave your children with. Trust your instincts and prioritize your child's safety above all. Open communication can make a world of difference in ensuring your child feels secure enough to share their feelings and experiences.

Let's come together to build a world where children feel safe and empowered to speak out. No child should ever feel like they have to carry such heavy burdens alone. Let's break the silence and support each other in healing.

Chapter Ten

The Meadows and the Bloods

You can't outrun the past, but you can try to outlive it.

The Meadows apartments were a huge change for our family. Up until then, we had always lived in houses—places with yards and space to breathe. But The Meadows were apartments, located on Meadowbrook on the East Side of Fort Worth, and everything about it felt different from where we had grown up. The South Side, where we had lived before, was Crip territory, known for its rough neighborhoods and the constant tension that came with it. But now we were in Blood territory, a place where the rules and culture were completely different.

At first, I didn't really understand the magnitude of it all. The South Side felt like home, even with the gang affiliation. It was where I knew the streets, the people, and the danger. But Meadowbrook—despite the obvious risks of gang culture—had a different vibe. Surprisingly, I found myself liking it better. The Bloods, while still tough, seemed friendlier in a way that I hadn't expected. Maybe it was just the change of scenery or the people I met, but there was something about this side of town that felt less hostile, even though it was still a dangerous place.

But the risk was always there. I wasn't in a gang myself, but being around my brothers' friends, who were often affiliated with gangs, meant I was always on the edge of trouble. I wasn't directly involved in the violence or the drama, but the lines were blurred. When you're hanging with the people your brothers associate with, you're always at risk of being caught up in something you didn't ask for. It didn't take much to end up in a dangerous situation.

We stayed at The Meadows for about six months before we were evicted. That period was chaotic, filled with moments of tension, uncertainty, and just trying to get by. The worst part wasn't even the eviction itself—it was how we had come to rely on that place, only to be pushed out. In a lot of ways, The Meadows represented both a fresh start and a harsh reminder of how quickly things could fall apart.

Kasey's decision to join the Bloods was one of those moments that felt both bold and reckless at the same time. At first, I didn't take it seriously. Kasey was always the type to do things his own way, and part of me thought it was just another one of his rebellious acts. He wanted to be part of something, and I couldn't say I was completely surprised by it. But when he made the move, it was like flipping a switch. Kasey wasn't just my older brother anymore—he was someone who had chosen a side in a war that had serious consequences.

I remember the first time I heard him talk about it. He was laughing, almost like he thought it was funny. But there was nothing funny about it, especially not when I started to see the reactions from people. Kasey had always been tough, but now he was wearing that red like a badge. And that's where things got tricky.

See, on the South Side where we came from, the color red wasn't just a color—it was a death sentence if you were wearing it in Crip territory. Red was "dead," a term they used to refer to the Bloods, their sworn enemies. The rivalry was so intense that you couldn't even mention the word "Blood" without facing hostility. Instead, they'd call them "floods." It was a subtle way of acknowledging them without ever using the forbidden "B" word. Red wasn't just a fashion choice—it was a declaration of war.

I thought it was bold at first. Kasey was fearless, but that decision almost cost us our lives.

I'll never forget the day in 1992 when I was twelve, and Kasey was thirteen, the day we transferred from Morningside Middle School to Meadowbrook Middle. It was supposed to be a fresh start, but Kasey's decision to walk into that school with those bright red gangsta Nikes—Nike Cortez, the ones that screamed gang affiliation—was anything but a fresh start. Instead of blending in, he was immediately marked.

As soon as we stepped onto the school grounds, I felt the weight of it. People started whispering. The tension was almost palpable. I didn't even have to ask what was going on—everyone was talking about the shoes. People came up to me, asking, "Why he got on them dead shoes?" It was like the whole school had a single thought on their mind. The shoes were more than just shoes; they were a symbol. A symbol of Kasey's decision to affiliate with the Bloods.

The hostility in the air was thick. I felt it as people looked at us, their eyes full of judgment, anger, and curiosity. But it wasn't just Kasey they were targeting.

I could feel the heat from their glares, too. As his little brother, I was linked to his choice, and I was already caught in the crossfire, whether I liked it or not. Kasey might've been fearless, but I wasn't stupid. I knew the consequences of his actions, and I could feel them creeping closer.

To them, those shoes were like a target painted on Kasey's back. I felt the tension building, but I didn't know what to do. The Crip culture didn't tolerate red, and by Kasey wearing those shoes, he was sending a message. That was when I realized the consequences of his actions weren't just personal—they could affect everyone around him.

It was bold, yes. But it was also dangerous.

And so, Kasey's decision to join the Bloods, to wear that red proudly, became a turning point. It was a choice that changed everything. Even though we lived in the Bloods' territory now, that didn't make it any safer. The rivalry between Crips and Bloods wasn't just about colors—it was about survival, and Kasey had just put us all in a situation where surviving wasn't guaranteed.

The danger wasn't just in the streets; it was in every move we made. Kasey thought he was being bold, showing the world he didn't care about the rules. But in doing so, he brought the danger right to our doorstep. And for me, that was a wake-up call.

Despite the underlying tensions, nobody dared to come near us or try anything at Morningside.

Meadowbrook turned out to be a bit of a surprise. The atmosphere there was different from what I expected. People were still wary of Kasey, sure, and his affiliation with the Bloods put a target on his back, but the general vibe at the school wasn't as hostile as I feared. It wasn't perfect by any means, but for some reason, I found myself enjoying the new environment. I didn't know if it was the fact that we were on the East Side, away from the constant drama of the South Side, or if it was the people I met, but something about it felt like a fresh chance.

Still, I couldn't shake the feeling that Kasey was constantly vulnerable. The risk was always there, lurking just beneath the surface. His affiliation with the Bloods meant that no matter where he went, he had to watch his back. The other kids at Meadowbrook might have been more laid-back, but outside those school walls, the streets of Meadowbrook were still filled with tension. One wrong move, one wrong word, and Kasey could find himself in deep trouble.

The reality was that Kasey had just put a giant target on his back. Every step he took, every decision he made, could potentially lead to something dangerous. And that's why, despite the somewhat positive experience at school, I couldn't forget how quickly things could turn south for him.

Being the younger brother of someone as popular and tough as Kasey had its perks, even though I didn't fully understand the weight of it all at the time. Kasey was cool. He had that presence, the kind of confidence that made people take notice. And honestly, I wanted to be seen with him. There was a certain status that came with being his brother, and deep down, I liked the idea of people seeing me as connected to someone so tough.

It was a typical afternoon when the bus pulled up to Meadowbrook Middle. I was supposed to ride home with the other kids, but when I saw Kasey standing outside with his friends, I felt that pull. I wanted to be near him, to be seen with him, to share that same aura of cool that seemed to follow him everywhere. So, I asked the bus driver if I could get off. "I'm going with my brother," I said, trying to sound casual, but there was an edge to my voice. The idea of walking with Kasey made me feel more connected, more important somehow.

I could tell the other kids on the bus had noticed Kasey and his friends too. They were pointing him out, whispering among themselves. "There go your brother," one of them said. It was like Kasey's popularity gave me a little boost, and I liked it. I wasn't used to that feeling, but it was addicting.

So, I stepped off the bus, walked over to him, and dapped him up. I avoided any gang-related handshakes or gestures, knowing that being even remotely connected to the wrong crowd could get me into serious trouble. But still, I wanted to be near him.

As we walked down the street, everything felt normal, even though I was hyper-aware of the danger. Then, just when I thought everything might be fine, a familiar car rolled up—an old blue two-door 1987 Oldsmobile Cutlass. I immediately recognized it. It was Carlos, someone I knew from the South Side. We'd crossed paths a few times before, and since he knew us, I thought, *this should be okay*. I didn't think for a second that anything bad would happen. Carlos was someone from our past, from my old neighborhood, and I figured he wouldn't mess with us.

I barely had a moment to react when Carlos got out of the car. There was no greeting, no warning, just his eyes locked onto Kasey and the rest of us. He popped open the trunk and, in one smooth motion, pulled out a 12-gauge shotgun. My heart sank.

Without any hesitation, Carlos pointed that shotgun at us and fired. The sound of the blast echoed through the street. Everything froze in that moment. My legs were rooted to the ground, but my mind was screaming to run. But where? I had nowhere to go. In a split second, I realized Kasey had disappeared. He bolted, running faster than I ever thought possible, disappearing into the chaos of the street. He was gone, and I was left standing there, terrified, alone behind that tree, watching as the world around me fell apart.

I was left alone. Frozen. A gust of wind rushed past me, but I didn't move. The shock paralyzed me. My eyes were wide, my breath caught in my chest, but the worst part was the overwhelming isolation that gripped me. I was behind that tree, hiding, unable to move, scared to even blink. Carlos wasn't looking my way, but the possibility that he might swing his gun toward me was enough to keep me paralyzed.

This was just the beginning of what would turn out to be a much more complicated, dangerous journey. The streets were always watching, and no matter how safe you felt in the moment, the danger was never far behind. I had wanted to walk with Kasey, to be seen with him, but now I realized that the price of that connection came with a heavy, deadly cost.

I could feel my heart pounding in my throat. That was real. That was *dangerous*. And it was happening *right now*.

It was all happening so fast. My mind was racing with a thousand thoughts, but one stood out above all: my red shoes. Those red Nikes—Kasey's bold fashion statement, the thing that had marked us before we even set foot in Meadowbrook. I had tried to tell myself they were just shoes, just a symbol of style, but in that moment, they weren't. They were the *wrong* shoes. The color was like a neon target on my back.

I wasn't stupid. I knew I had to hide them. My heart was pounding in my chest as I looked down, but there was nowhere to run, nowhere to hide. I didn't have time to think about anything other than the fact that those shoes were the reason Carlos could've turned that shotgun on me, too. I ducked lower behind the tree, trying to conceal my feet, hoping against all hope that Carlos wouldn't notice.

The shame and fear twisted in my gut. I felt exposed, vulnerable. The red shoes weren't just a fashion statement; they were a death sentence if the wrong person saw them.

I could hear Carlos's footsteps growing distant, but my fear of him turning around to finish what he started kept me glued to that tree, unable to move, praying he wouldn't come back.

Kasey was gone, long disappeared into the maze of streets and alleyways. I had no idea where he went or if he was okay, but the fact that I was still alive was a miracle.

I don't know how long I stayed there, hiding behind that tree, waiting for the danger to pass. Time seemed to stretch, and the air felt heavier with every breath I took. But eventually, it was clear Carlos had left. The sound of his car driving away in the distance brought a brief flicker of relief.

I didn't waste any time. I got up and ran as fast as I could, my red shoes barely making a sound on the pavement. The only thing in my mind was getting home. Home felt like the safest place in the world. I made my way through the streets, trying not to look over my shoulder. Every step felt like a countdown until I would hear that screeching car, or worse, see Carlos coming for me. But I made it home.

When I finally walked through that door, it felt like a heavy weight lifted off my chest. I didn't even realize how tense I'd been until I stepped inside, feeling the warmth of the house and the safety of it. I wanted to collapse, but I was too shaken to let myself break down.

Kevin was already there when I walked in. His eyes immediately locked onto me, scanning me from head to toe. He knew something had gone wrong.

"Where's Kasey?" Kevin asked, his voice steady but with an undercurrent of worry.

I didn't have an answer for him—not the one he wanted. I just shook my head. The reality of what had happened was starting to settle in, and I wasn't sure if I had the words to explain it. I'd never seen Kevin like this before. His expression was a blend of anger and worry, and it was obvious he understood just how serious the situation was.

"You don't get it, do you, Randy?" Kevin's voice was low, intense. "That *was* a warning. You're too close to this, man. One of these days, it's gonna catch up with you. And when it does, it won't be easy."

The weight of his words hit me like a ton of bricks. Kevin wasn't just talking about Carlos or the incident. He was talking about the entire lifestyle Kasey had stepped into—the dangers, the unpredictability, the violence that was always lurking in the background. Kevin had seen the consequences before, and he was right.

The reality of what I had just experienced—the gunfire, the hiding, the near-death situation—was sinking in. I wasn't just the little brother anymore. I was part of it, whether I liked it or not. This was a world of danger, and now I was tied to it, whether I wanted to be or not.

As I tried to process everything that had just happened, the overwhelming feeling was fear. Fear of what had happened and fear of what was yet to come. Fear that Kasey's choices were pulling me deeper into a world I wasn't prepared for.

But more than fear, I felt loyalty. Loyalty to my brother. It was an instinct, an unspoken bond that I couldn't shake, no matter how dangerous or reckless his decisions might seem. It was the kind of loyalty that made me want to stand by him, even when the world around us was falling apart.

But that loyalty came with a cost.

I knew now that the streets weren't just about who you hung out with—they were about survival. And survival in this world meant making choices. Hard choices. Choices that could get you killed.

As I thought about what had happened, I couldn't help but realize that this was just one of many experiences that would change my life. I had seen how the streets could affect people and their families. I understood that Kasey's choices, whether good or bad, were already starting to change my life in ways I wasn't ready for.

This was just the beginning. The road ahead was unclear, and the results of Kasey's decisions—our decisions—were waiting for us. It was a world where fear, loyalty, and choices mattered the most. I wasn't sure if we would get through this without getting hurt.

Chapter Eleven

A Big Fight

The greatest battle you will ever fight is the battle within yourself.

When we moved to the Meadows, I wasn't sure where Kevin was living, but one thing I knew for sure—he didn't want to be anywhere near that side of town. He'd show up every now and then, often bragging about the cars he'd stolen. He'd park them outside, proud of whatever he'd swiped that week. But it wasn't just the cars that seemed to define Kevin during those days—it was the chaos that followed him around.

Things started to get worse for all of us when Kasey made his decision to switch gangs. In our world, that was called "flip-flopping" or "selling out." And let me tell you—nothing is more embarrassing than watching your own family make a move like that. It wasn't just about Kasey; it was about all of us. The Moore name was getting stained, and for Kevin, that was a blow to his pride. He was supposed to be the tough one, the one who didn't take any nonsense, and now his little brother was dragging their name through the mud.

The pressure on Kevin was insane. Everywhere we went, people whispered about Kasey's flip, and the embarrassment hit Kevin hard. It wasn't just the gang culture that messed us up—it was the reputation, the judgment from everyone around us. And that pressure? It broke out into a fight between Kevin and Kasey. A huge one. So big that the landlord decided it was time for us to leave. We weren't wanted there anymore, and to be honest, I don't think anyone blamed the landlord. The place was falling apart, and with the family in constant turmoil, it was only a matter of time before we were out.

The reality of it all? We didn't have much of a choice when it came to moving. Our money situation was tight. Grama relied on her Social Security and disability checks, while momma relied on our welfare check, and if those didn't come through, we couldn't even think about moving. We didn't have savings or a backup plan. So when it was time to leave, it had to be done around the 1st or the 3rd of the month—whenever the checks came in.

But Grama, she always found a way. We packed up and made our way to this big blue house on Victory Drive. It was in the Polytechnic Heights area of Fort Worth, Texas. This was a different part of town, southeast of the city, and I wasn't sure what to expect. The neighborhood had a lot of landmarks—Polytechnic High School, Texas Wesleyan University, and Sycamore Park. I was in the 8th grade by then, trying to get my head around all the changes.

When we first moved, it was me, my mom, Grama, my Uncle Michael, Brandon, and Leisa. Kasey went to live with his dad, and Kevin was in and out. I could tell Kevin wasn't fully settled either. He'd show up, but it wasn't like before. It wasn't the same.

School was a whole other battle. By the time we moved to Victory Drive, I'd missed a ton of school. But I wasn't like Brandon and Leisa. They didn't care about school—most people didn't. But for me, school was my escape. It was the only chance I had to get out of the mess we were in. If I didn't make it, I'd end up just like my Uncle Michael, stuck living with my mom and Grama forever. I couldn't do that.

It wasn't easy, though. I had these red Nike Cortez shoes that weren't even mine— they belonged to Wayne, one of Kasey's friends. He'd asked to borrow my shoes, and I never got them back. No one told me it was a bad idea to wear them. I thought it was just shoes—who cared, right? But those red shoes? They made me an instant target.

Money was tight, so I couldn't just go out and buy new ones. I had to get creative. I asked Grama for bus money so I could still get to school. I was about thirteen in 1993, and I'd never ridden the city bus before. But I figured it out. I took the bus to downtown Fort Worth, transferred, and ended up at Meadowbrook every day.

Then one day, I got on the wrong bus. Instead of ending up at Meadowbrook, I was dropped off deep in Crip territory on Miller Avenue. And there I was—wearing my red shoes. Panic hit me like a freight train. I had no idea what to do. I ducked behind a rock, hiding my shoes, praying I wouldn't get caught.

Later, Kevin's friend told me that he saw me there. Apparently, he had "yoked it", made a U-turn, to check out who I was, but when he recognized I was "Kevin's brother", he let me go. I swear, that day felt like I was being watched over. It was like God had His hand on me.

Eventually, I got the hang of the bus routes and started making it to school every day. But back home, Brandon and Leisa still didn't care. They weren't motivated like me. They'd call me stupid for going to school, but I knew what was at stake. I knew it was my only way out.

So that's where we were—still figuring it out, trying to survive, and hoping that somehow things would get better. But they didn't always get better. Not for any of us.

When we moved into that blue house on Victory Drive, we had a lot of things to figure out. The first problem? Getting the lights and gas turned on. The electricity? No problem. But the gas? It was another story. They couldn't turn it on right away, and winter was creeping up fast. And let me tell you, winter in Texas might not be as cold as up north, but when you don't have heat, it feels like it's freezing.

It got bad. We had to huddle together in Grama's room, where she had this old electric heater that barely worked. The rest of the house? It was freezing. I remember stepping outside of her room, and it felt like stepping into an icebox. We made pallets on the floor, bundled up in every blanket we could find, and just tried to survive. It was rough. But Grama, she kept it together. She made sure we didn't freeze. Somehow, she always did.

One Thanksgiving, I was sure we wouldn't have anything to eat, but lo and behold, Grama walked in with a big box filled with prepared food; all we had to do was warm it up on the hot plates that we had. It was a miracle, really, and I could hardly believe my eyes. The aroma of turkey and stuffing filled the air, making our cramped little house feel warm and inviting, if only for a moment.

Despite all we went through at this house, we had some good memories. The swing set in the backyard was where Brandon, Leisa, and I used to play, our laughter ringing out like music. Kevin would come over, and we'd spend hours rapping Tupac, Snoop Dogg, and Dr. Dre, losing ourselves in the rhythm and the words. Those moments felt like a different life, one where worries didn't creep in as often, and I don't remember Momma going out to do drugs during those times.

As the nights grew colder, we turned to each other for warmth—not just physically, but emotionally. In those moments, the chill didn't matter. We were together, creating our own heat through shared memories. Grama listened, her eyes twinkling with a mix of nostalgia and pride, reminding us that we were stronger together.

One night, as the wind howled outside, she leaned back in her chair, wrapped in a blanket and began to share tales from her younger days, stories filled with courage.

She told us about the time she had jumped out of a burning building, her voice steady despite the gravity of the memory. "I was young and scared, but I knew I had to get me and my kids out," she recounted, her eyes distant as if she were reliving that moment. "I landed hard and broke my hip but made it. That taught me that sometimes you have to take a leap of faith, even if it's scary."

We listened intently, our imaginations painting vivid pictures of her bravery. Grama's stories were like a warm embrace, wrapping around our hearts and reminding us that strength could be found in the most unexpected places.

Then she spoke of her daughter, a name that felt like a ghost in our family history. "Your mother has a sister," she revealed gently, "someone you've never met. She was taken from me many years ago, but she was a beautiful little girl." Her voice trembled slightly, and we could sense the weight of loss that had lingered with her all these years. "Life took her in a different direction, but she always held a piece of my heart."

The room fell silent, each of us grasping this new piece of our family's history. It was a moment of connection, a reminder that our struggles were not isolated but part of a larger story that extended beyond the walls of our blue house.

In that silence, we felt a bond deepening among us. We might not have had a perfect life, but we had each other—and the memories we shared, both joyful and painful, knit us closer together. Grama's strength was a beacon, guiding us through our own challenges, and her stories illuminated paths we could take, even when the way felt dark and uncertain.

While we were dealing with that, I knew I had to keep going to school. It was my way out. I'd already missed so much school because of all the moving around, and I couldn't afford to miss any more. For most people, dropping out was no big deal, but I knew that if I didn't stay in school, I'd end up stuck in the same cycle my family had been in for years.

As I think back, I am surprised that the adults were so comfortable with how we lived. I was only thirteen, but they had been doing this same thing—moving from house to house, living from paycheck to paycheck, dropping out of school—same ole same ole for years. How did they not want better for their kids? Why did they not see the cycle that was continuing? Why was no one willing to break this cycle?

I often found myself questioning their choices, wrestling with the confusion of being a kid who could see the cracks in our lives while the adults seemed to accept them as normal. It was as if they had grown accustomed to the chaos, the instability, and the struggle, believing it was simply how life was meant to be. Maybe they had lost hope in the possibility of something better, or perhaps they were so consumed by their own battles that they couldn't envision a different future for us.

There were nights when I'd lie awake, staring at the ceiling, pondering these thoughts. I remember watching Grama as she sat in her chair, her hands weathered and tired, and I could see the weight of the world resting on her shoulders. She had fought her own battles, and perhaps in her heart, she felt that fighting for change was too daunting.

And then there were the moments when I saw my mother, her eyes glazed over, lost in thoughts that were too heavy for a kid like me to understand. I wanted to shake her, to tell her that there was more to life than this. But I also understood that sometimes, the pain of the past can be a heavy anchor, weighing you down and making it hard to dream of a different life.

It was frustrating, struggling with the realization that the very adults who were supposed to guide us were stuck in a cycle they didn't seem to recognize. I wanted to scream, to make them see the future we could have, if only they would fight for it. But instead, we were left to navigate our own paths through the shadows they cast.

Yet, within that frustration, a spark ignited in me. I felt a sense of responsibility, not only for myself but for Leisa and Brandon. I wanted to break the cycle, to create a different narrative for us. I began to dream of a life where we would have more than just survival; we would have hope, education, and opportunities.

It became clear to me that while the adults might have accepted this way of life, we didn't have to. We could choose to be different, to strive for better, and to lift each other up. I knew it wouldn't be easy, but with every story shared by Grama, every laugh echoed in the backyard, and every moment of unity we created, we were building the foundation for a brighter future.

The realization that changes could start with us became a powerful driving force. I promised myself that I would do everything I could to break the cycle, to lift us out of the shadows, and to ensure that our story would be one of strength and hope, rather than one of defeat.

We didn't stay on Victory Drive for too long. Eventually, Momma and Grama were approved to move into the Glen Garden apartments, and there we were, moving back to the deep South Side of Fort Worth. I remember Kevin and my Uncle Michael getting so excited about moving back, but I was not so thrilled.

When we first moved to Glen Garden, it felt somewhat familiar since we knew most of the people in the area, and many of them knew Kevin and Kasey, so I felt secure. It was like stepping back into a world I had known.

I soon encountered a kid named Demarkus, whose family was known to be the tough crew in the apartments. I was around thirteen and in the 8th grade by then. Having been bullied by the kid Lawrence and having had a couple of fights, including with Joseph and the kid who cut his leg—I knew I wasn't about to let anyone run over me.

This kid Demarkus couldn't have been more than ten or eleven, but he had a way of provoking me that felt all too familiar. One day, something snapped inside me, and I jumped at him as if I were going to punch him. His eyes widened, and he quickly responded, "I'm going to go get my uncle." I felt a mix of adrenaline and uncertainty as I walked back from the little corner store by the apartments, which we called Mr. Moon's after the owner.

In that moment, just as I was trying to shake off the tension, his uncle rounded the corner. He looked to be about 25, and his name was Robert. The air felt thick with anticipation, and I braced myself, thinking I might be in for a fight. But just as it seemed like he was about to unleash his anger on me, I said, "Let me go get my brother."

He paused, confusion flickering across his face. "Who is your brother?" he asked. Without missing a beat, I replied, "Kevin." The effect was instantaneous; it was as if a switch had been flipped. Robert's demeanor changed completely, shifting from hostility to something more friendly and even respectful. From that moment, we all became the best of friends, a bond formed under the strangest of circumstances.

While I was at Mr. Moon's getting a jungle juice later that week, I noticed a man in line who looked very familiar. I stared hard at him, and he walked up to me, saying, "What's up, little man! Yeah, it's me." It was Lawrence, the van driver who had bought me my first pair of church shoes. I was surprised to see him there, and it brought back memories of that time. It was a strange yet comforting feeling to run into someone from my past in a new place, a reminder of how connected our lives could be, even during chaos.

When we moved back to the South Side, Kasey came to live with us again. We were all crammed into a two-bedroom apartment until Momma got her own place, but that didn't last. Kasey had become a Blood, and he was going to have to pay for that decision. He stayed in the house with me, and while I was okay with it, I also felt the weight of my promise to myself. I was determined not to follow in Kevin and Kasey's footsteps and was committed to breaking the family cycle.

Kasey was paranoid, and he had every right to be. One day, a large group of Crips came to our house after they found out Kasey was inside. My heart raced as I realized the danger we were in once again.

As I watched the scene unfold, worry gripped me. Kasey had already run off and left me before; I wasn't sure how he would handle this situation. But Kevin arrived just in time, standing tall and firm. "This ain't happening," he declared, making it clear that if they were going to fight Kasey, they would have to fight all of us.

To my surprise and relief, the Crips forgave Kasey that day. Perhaps it was the presence of Kevin, or maybe they recognized the bond we shared as a family. Whatever the reason, Kasey was back in the game.

Living in that apartment, surrounded by familiar faces and new challenges, I felt the weight of our choices pressing down on us. I was determined to carve out a different path, to find a way to navigate through the chaos without getting swept away by it. Each day was a lesson, a reminder that breaking the cycle wouldn't be easy, but with every challenge faced together, I felt a flicker of hope that maybe, just maybe, we could redefine our story.

Chapter Twelve

September 1994

No one can hear the weight of your past or the echo of your dreams.

The night was thick with heat, the kind that made you feel like you couldn't breathe, but we didn't mind. We were up in the apartment, hanging out with friends, laughing and talking about nothing important. Life felt normal for once. But then, everything changed in an instant.

Kevin burst into the room like a hasty, his face pale with panic. "Get down! Turn off the lights!" he shouted. His voice cracked, like he knew something was about to happen. We didn't ask questions. We dropped to the floor, our hearts pounding, as the sound of gunfire cracked through the air. It wasn't a single shot, but a string of them, fast and chaotic, like the world was unraveling outside our window.

My eyes darted to the window, and I saw it—familiar headlights flashing in the darkness. A car. We didn't know who was driving it, but we knew that it wasn't just anyone. And then, the sound of tires screeching and people running, fading quickly into the night. The chaos was over as fast as it had started.

I was still on the floor, shaking. "It came from Lawrence's place," Kevin whispered, his voice tight. "You need to check on him."

Kevin knew what just happened; Lawrence had been robbed, and the likelihood of him being hurt or worse loomed heavy in the air. He knew that Lawrence and I shared a long history, a bond that was built on trust. There was no way Lawrence would ever harm me. Yet, as much as he urged me to go, I could see the hesitation in Kevin's eyes.

He didn't want to go check on Lawrence himself, and it became clear why. His friends were likely the ones behind the robbery, and there was a real fear that Lawrence might mistake Kevin for one of them. It was my job to "check on him," but Kevin had also layered his request with other instructions: "Make sure to grab some money." It was a strange mix of concern for Lawrence's safety and a desire to ensure we had what we needed in the chaos that had just unfolded.

I rushed downstairs, my mind racing. The apartment felt eerily quiet, too quiet, like the calm before the storm. I made my way over to the building next door, walking cautiously, one foot in front of the other, as if I could somehow slow time down. When I reached Lawrence's door, I saw it. The door had been kicked in, the frame splintered, and right next to it was the unmistakable imprint of a Converse shoe. Someone had been in a hurry.

I stepped forward, my heart thudding in my chest. "Lawrence?" I called out softly. "It's me, Randy."

The response was immediate, and it hit me like a punch to the gut. "Man, help me!"

I froze.

There he was, lying on the floor. His body was twisted in pain, two bullet holes in his chest, blood staining the carpet. The room around him was a mess—money scattered across the floor, marijuana bags spilling from a table. It looked like a robbery gone wrong. But that didn't matter to me. What mattered was Lawrence, the man who once told me to go to church, the man who had always been kind to me, lying there, slowly dying.

His eyes were glassy, his breath shallow. He was still alive, but barely. I dropped to my knees beside him, panic rising in my throat. Without thinking, I grabbed a towel from the counter and pressed it against his chest, trying to stop the bleeding. The 911 operator's voice echoed in my mind, telling me what to do, but nothing felt real. The only thing I could think of was how this man, the "Weed Man," who had once tried to lead me to a better life, was now fighting for his own.

The weight of it hit me. Lawrence wasn't just some guy I knew; he was a part of something bigger. He had a life outside of this, a life I didn't even know. And now, that life was slipping away. I should've done more. I should've been there sooner.

I pressed harder on Lawrence's chest, my hands trembling with panic. The 911 operator's voice was distant, almost drowned out by the pounding in my ears. "Apply pressure to the wound," she had said. But what she hadn't told me was how the pressure would feel like an endless weight, crushing me as much as it was trying to stop the bleeding.

I could hear her voice in the background, giving me step-by-step instructions, but none of it felt real. My mind was spiraling, filled with confusion, fear, and a sense of helplessness I'd never felt before. I should've been thinking more clearly, should've followed the advice to toss the money out the window, to make the scene look different. But Lawrence was dying in front of me, and nothing else mattered in that moment. I could only focus on keeping him alive, praying that somehow, the towel I pressed against his chest would make a difference.

His breath was coming in shallow gasps now, each one weaker than the last. I tried to stay calm, tried to stay strong, but the reality of the situation hit me with the force of a freight train. This wasn't just some accident. This was a life taken in the blink of an eye, and there was nothing I could do to stop it.

I couldn't get the image of his face out of my mind—the man who had once encouraged me to go to church, the one who bought me my first pair of dress shoes. And now, here he was, a victim of the same chaos that had consumed so many others in our neighborhood. Lawrence had lived two lives, each pulling him in opposite directions. The man who had once given me guidance had now become part of the very world he had tried to help me escape. And in the end, it had cost him everything.

By the time the paramedics arrived, I knew it was too late. He was still alive, but just barely. The paramedics took over, and I left the scene as the police came and went. Before the night ended, there was yellow police tape everywhere, and soon I found out that Lawrence had died.

It was hard to believe that this man, who used to be a van driver for the church and always encouraged me, had given all that up to sell weed. The people he sold to had turned on him, and that felt so unfair. I thought, "What a cruel world." If the church created people like him, I started to wonder if I wanted anything to do with it. The good feelings I once had began to fade away, replaced by the sadness of what happened to Lawrence.

As the years passed, the memory of that night stayed with me like a heavy shadow, never fully leaving. The faces of the men who took Lawrence's life were now known, their names printed in the newspapers, their arrests a bitter twist of justice that did little to erase the pain. But there was no peace in that. There was no closure.

What haunted me the most wasn't just the brutal way Lawrence had died, or the way his life had slipped between the cracks of a world that didn't care. It was the feeling that his death was just the beginning. A part of me couldn't shake the nagging suspicion that Lawrence's fate was a warning, not just for him, but for all of us.

I'd already lost so much, and yet, here I was, still watching it unfold. Another friend taken. Another life lost to the cruel cycle that seemed inescapable. The weight of it all pressed down on me, harder with each passing day, like the world was slowly suffocating everything good that had ever been in it.

I couldn't help but wonder how many more would fall. How many more would be swallowed up by the violence, the drugs, and the desperation that filled the air we breathed. Lawrence had been just another casualty, but the truth was, none of us were safe. None of us had a way out. Not really.

Standing there in the quiet, I realized just how small we all were in a world so much bigger than us, and how easily a life could be snuffed out. There were no heroes here, no easy answers, just the raw, unfiltered reality of survival.

And though I tried to move on, tried to push the image of Lawrence's final moments out of my head, the truth was inescapable. The harshness of this world—our world—had taken another friend. And deep down, I knew this wouldn't be the last. Not by a long shot.

Lawrence's death was just the beginning.

And the darkness? It was only getting closer.

Chapter Thirteen

Glen Garden's History

Why it is mandatory to repeat the history?

I sat at the kitchen table, a plate of buttered toast in front of me, the smell of coffee lingering in the air. The morning light filtered through the window, casting soft shadows across the room. I took a bite of my toast, chewing slowly, my eyes drifting outside. The sight of children playing in the street caught my attention. They were laughing, running in the sun like everything was right in the world, like nothing had ever gone wrong.

For a moment, I was lost in their laughter, in that carefree joy that seemed so far away from the life I'd come to know. I could almost hear the echoes of my own laughter from when I was their age—me and my brothers and cousins, racing down the street, the world seeming so simple back then. We were just kids, not yet touched by the mess that would follow.

But then, without warning, the memory slipped away, and something darker began to creep in. The laughter of the children outside started to blur, replaced by a faint hum—a sound I knew too well: the distant wail of sirens. It cut through the warmth of the morning like an icy chill, pulling me back to a time when everything changed.

It was just a few days after Lawrence's death when the night took a turn for the worse. Shots rang out again, breaking the silence, but thankfully, this time no one was killed. I lay on the floor of our apartment, surrounded by darkness. The window was open, letting in a cool breeze that felt good against the heat that filled the air.

The water had been off in the complex for weeks, and now the lights were out too, making everything feel even more empty. I could hear voices from across the street, and soon an argument broke out. Then, I heard the loud sound of gunfire. My heart raced, and fear crept in as I tried to understand what was happening outside.

As I lay there on the cold floor, I couldn't help but think, "Could things get any worse?" The darkness felt heavy around me, reminding me of how tough our situation was. In that moment, I realized that danger felt like it was always just a heartbeat away.

Glen Garden had its own troubled history. Back in 1967, while the apartments were being built, a three-alarm fire destroyed the eight-unit Glen Garden Apartments at 1200 Glen Garden Drive, resulting in an estimated $30,000 loss. At that time, the project was still in the early stages, with wooden frameworks and some sheetrock in place. Glen Garden was the last apartment complex on the north side of the block, right across from Morningside Middle School.

Fast forward 27 years to 1994, just days after Lawrence's death. A dispute over ownership of the apartments had left many low-income and elderly residents without water. A newspaper article described the situation occurring "amid the sweltering September heat," yet no one came to help us.

Apparently, the owners were in a dispute over who held the title. In the midst of this argument, they had fallen $17,000 behind on their water bills, leaving all the tenants without water.

On the 1st and the 3rd of the month, everyone would gather by the mailbox, waiting for their welfare, Social Security, and SSI disability checks. I despised that scene. Most of the people on welfare were women struggling with drug addiction, and the money rarely benefited the children—the drug dealers were the real winners. The elderly folks on Social Security or SSI were the ones holding everything together.

By the time the 10th arrived, when this dispute occurred, everyone was out of money. One man told the newspaper, "I ain't got money to move." He was 54, a diabetic double amputee in a wheelchair. His rent was $400 a month, and he had already paid it, just like everyone else. We were all broke and didn't have the luxury to just pick up and relocate until the 1st came around again.

Later, I read a newspaper quote from a woman at the water department stating, "They've left the tenants high and dry… I've never heard of that." No one had ever intentionally shut off water in occupied apartment complexes. The Water Department manager at the time said they were instructed to cut off the water by the owners, claiming the complex was set to close and that residents had been given written notices to move out, but this was far from the truth.

One woman had just moved in on September 2nd, and she was quoted saying, "I've got three daughters and a grandbaby, and it's terrible sitting up here with no water." On top of that, she couldn't even get a mailbox key to retrieve her Social Security check. This wasn't the worst part. Despite being covered by the news, two weeks later, the electricity was cut off in the entire apartment complex, and no one came to help. People were shot, raped, killed, robbed—everything imaginable. Families with children, women, and elderly people were living in America as if they were in a war zone, and nobody intervened. They knew what was happening because it had been reported in the newspaper, on television, and police had responded to shootings and robberies. I could never comprehend this.

I felt the full weight of their neglect, as though the world had abandoned us. It was as if we were invisible to everyone outside their little corner of the world. The system that was supposed to protect us, to help us, had let us down. The streets of Glen Garden were a harsh reminder that survival wasn't just about getting by—it was about holding on to any shred of dignity you could find in a place that had long since stopped caring.

I remember those days well—the unbearable heat of late summer, the frustration in the air, the constant worry. The fire hydrants were the only source of water, until the Fire Department arrived, closing it off. People would stand in line, waiting their turn with buckets and jugs, just to get enough water to wash their clothes, cook, or flush the toilet. There was something degrading about it, like we were being forced to live in a way that wasn't even human, but it was the only option we had. And it was the elderly, the disabled, and the single mothers who bore the brunt of it all. They had nowhere else to go.

The authorities? Nowhere to be found. Even with the newspapers covering the story, with the cameras rolling and reporters talking about the injustice, no one came to help. It was like they'd all decided that Glen Garden wasn't worth saving, that we weren't worth saving.

We were living on borrowed time, though. Every day was a struggle, every moment of peace was temporary. The violence, the drugs, the constant fear — everything around us was pushing us further into despair. No one could escape it, not even the kids. In 1994, when tensions were already at their breaking point, the ownership dispute took the last bit of hope away. The water was shut off for twenty days, the lights were off for two weeks, and the residents were left scrambling to survive.

I'd see them — families trying to make do, their faces worn and tired, just like mine. They tried to keep things normal for their kids, but the environment around them made it impossible. How could they protect their children from what was happening to the world they lived in? When everything around you is a reminder of what's broken, it's hard to pretend that things are okay.

I watched my grandmother and the other elderly women try to maintain some semblance of normal life, even though it was slipping away. They made do with what they could, like when we'd have to go out in the dead of night just to try to get some water from a fire hydrant. But that wasn't living; it was survival. And when the system, the authorities, the very people who were supposed to help us—turned their backs, it became clear. The community of Glen Garden wasn't just living in physical decay, it was living in social decay, and there wasn't any real way out.

We were caught in a cycle, a trap that we couldn't escape. It felt like every generation before me had faced the same battles, and nothing ever changed.

By the time 1994 came around, I had already seen enough. I had lived through more than my fair share of hardships, but the feeling that nothing would ever improve—it started to settle in deep. I could feel it creeping up on me, the reality that maybe this was all we were ever going to get. And that was a tough pill to swallow.

I thought about Lawrence, about how he used to encourage me to go to church, about the way he had once been someone to look up to. Now he was just another victim of this messed-up world we had inherited. His death—like so many others—was part of the larger story of how Glen Garden had eaten us all alive. And yet, here I was, still trying to make sense of it all. But there was no making sense of it.

The system had failed us. The people who should have cared, the ones who were supposed to protect us—they had abandoned us. And now, all we had were our memories and the broken pieces of a community that was never given a chance to heal. It wasn't just about surviving anymore—it was about holding onto whatever bit of hope you could find, even if it meant pretending that things weren't as bad as they were. Because if you stopped pretending, if you really let yourself see how messed up it all was, then it would be over. You wouldn't be able to keep going.

And that was the hardest part—realizing that maybe, just maybe, Glen Garden had already lost. Maybe we had already lost.

School wasn't any better. For a while, I tried to hold onto some kind of normalcy—tried to stay focused on school. But it was impossible. How could I concentrate on algebra or history when I didn't know where my next meal was coming from, or when the lights might get turned off again? My 8th-grade graduation should have been something to be proud of, but I couldn't even attend because I didn't have a white shirt to wear. I still remember standing across the street, watching my classmates walk into the gym, knowing I wasn't one of them, knowing I didn't fit in. I felt like an outsider in my own life.

Even when I did go to school, I couldn't escape the constant reminder of where I came from. It wasn't just the fact that I couldn't afford the right clothes—it was the way people looked at me.

As the years went by, I began to realize that school, education, all that talk about the future—it wasn't for me. It wasn't for people like me. It felt like an illusion, a dream I wasn't ever meant to reach. I dropped out of school, like so many others around me. What was the point? The world outside Glen Garden didn't care about me. So why should I care about something that felt so far away from everything I was living through?

Mother Tosses 3 Children To Safety, Injured in Leap

A 20-year-old Negro mother threw three smal children from the third story of a flaming building at 612 Missouri Friday afternoon and then was injured as she leaped into waiting arms below.

The woman, Faye Evelyn Moore, received a fractured pelvis in her fall and was admitted to City-County Hospital in fair condition.

Her two sons, Lawrence, 4, and Dickie, 2, and another child, James Edward Tatum, 5, were treated for abrasions and released from the hospital.

The two-alarm fire swept through the top floor of the three-story rooming house, causing an estimated $4,500 damage. The cause was undetermined.

The fire department said the building is owned by May Turner.

In 1996, Glen Garden was reopened. But when I saw it, I didn't feel relief. It was like looking at a bandaged wound that had never healed properly. Sure, they rebuilt the walls, replaced the windows, fixed up the place to make it look livable again. But the cracks in the foundation weren't just physical—they were deeper, rooted in the history of the place. It wasn't just the apartments that had fallen apart—it was the community, the spirit of the people who lived there. Some of the same faces I saw before they closed in 1994 ultimately returned; the same pain, the same struggles. The rebuilding wasn't enough. It never would be.

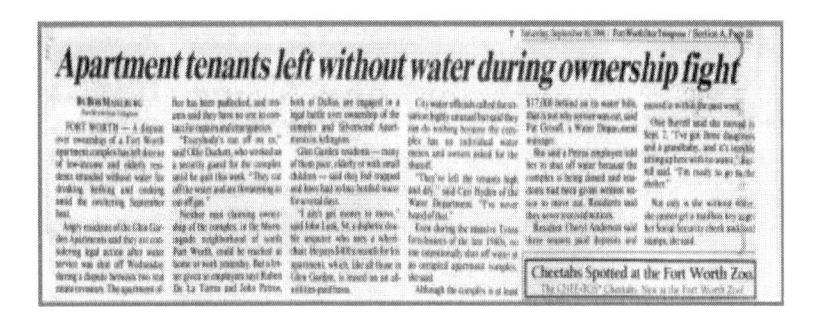

Apartment tenants left without water during ownership fight

Looking at the world outside Glen Garden, I started to see the truth in a new light. People who lived in better neighborhoods, people who didn't have to worry about gang violence or drug deals in the street, they didn't understand. They didn't care. They went about their lives as if nothing was wrong, as if people like me didn't even exist. But we did. We existed, and we were drowning in a world that didn't even know we were here.

Lawrence's death haunted me, too. I couldn't get rid of the memory of him, lying there with two bullet holes in his chest, the life fading from his eyes. He had been one of the few people who tried to push me to do better, to get out of the mess that was in Glen Garden. But even he couldn't escape it. I didn't understand it at the time, but I do now: violence, drugs, crime—those things weren't just random acts. They were the result of a broken system, a world that had no place for people like Lawrence, like me. I wanted answers. I wanted to know why violence was so ingrained in our world, why it felt like we were trapped in a never-ending cycle. But the truth was, I didn't have the answers. And I'm not sure I ever will.

As I stood on the edge of adulthood, I felt like I was standing on the edge of something much bigger than myself. The pain and trauma of the past haunted me, but it also made me stronger. I had survived, somehow, but I wasn't sure for how much longer I could keep going. Somewhere inside, I knew I had to keep pushing, had to keep fighting. But for the first time, I wondered—was there ever a way out? Or was I just going to be stuck in this cycle forever, watching the world change around me while I stayed the same?

I didn't have the answers, but I knew one thing for sure: I wasn't done yet. The fight wasn't over. But I couldn't shake the feeling that, no matter how far I'd come, I still hadn't figured it all out. The darkness of the past still hung over me, and I wasn't sure how much longer I could carry it.

Chapter Fourteen

The Projects

Poverty is the parent of revolution and crime.

I can still remember the day Kevin got sent to juvenile detention. He was fifteen and it wasn't even for something that he actually did, but sometimes life works that way, doesn't it? A small mistake, a split-second decision, and everything changes.

I was sitting on the porch, just thinking about my brother, the one who'd always been my protector. Kevin was the one who'd taught me how to fight, how to hustle, and how to survive. He was my hero back then, even if I didn't always show it. When I think back to those days, it feels like a lifetime ago. But it wasn't. It was just yesterday in my mind.

I remember the fights we used to have, and some of them were pretty intense. There was that one time over the socks that Kevin swore I lost. It escalated quickly, and before I knew it, we were out in the street. He punched me right in the eye before I could even throw a hit back. He hit me so hard that my vision blurred for a moment. An ambulance was called to make sure I was okay, but I wasn't taken to the hospital. True to his nature, Kevin never offered an apology. Instead, he came into the room, laid on the bed beside me, and pulled my hand off my face, saying, "Let me see." To me, that was all the reassurance I needed.

Then there was another fight over a coat we both wanted. It turned into such a serious brawl that Kevin ended up with a stab wound in his back. Once again, the ambulance was called, and this time he was taken to the ER for stitches. Kevin swore I had stabbed him, but I knew I hadn't. Even though I wasn't to blame, I felt hurt because he was hurt. Just like before, no words of apology were exchanged. Instead, I took care of his wound every day, and that's all he needed from me. Our bond was complicated, filled with fights and love, but at the end of the day, we always found a way to show we cared for each other.

It always felt like I was fighting for respect, for some kind of recognition, even though I never really understood why. Kevin was always there to back me up, even when he was in the wrong. But the day he got sent away, it wasn't about respect. It was about something darker. A mess that was bigger than both of us.

In Fort Worth, Texas, there stood a place known as the Ripley Arnold Projects. Located near the corner of Belknap Street, this public housing development was built in the 1940s to help families in need of affordable homes. The projects were named after Ripley Arnold, a man who played an important role in the city's history.

After World War II, many people returned home to find that there weren't enough houses for everyone. Families struggled to find safe and comfortable places to live. The Ripley Arnold Projects were created to solve this problem. They included several apartment buildings where low-income families could find shelter. Among those families were many African American families who faced unfair treatment when trying to find homes.

At first, the Ripley Arnold Projects offered hope and a fresh start for many families. Children played in the parks, and neighbors helped each other out. However, as time went on, the projects faced many challenges. The buildings began to fall into disrepair, and safety became a concern. Some people started to see the Ripley Arnold Projects as a place filled with problems, not the community it had once been.

In the 1970s, the Ripley Arnold Projects were a true blessing for my grandmother. She was raising my mother and uncle on her own, struggling to make ends meet. The housing offered by the projects provided them with a safe place to live during tough times. As my mother grew up and started her own family, she eventually got her own apartment in the projects.

Years later, we moved out of the projects, but it was interesting how history seemed to repeat itself. My brothers, Kevin and Kasey, often hung out in those familiar streets, and I wanted to join them. But they usually wouldn't let me come along.

The projects were filled with stories of our family, both good and bad, and while it felt like home, it was also dangerous. Kevin and Kasey wanted to keep me safe, knowing the risks that came with returning to that environment. I could see the tension in their eyes when they talked about it, and I understood that they were trying to protect me from the same struggles they faced growing up. Even though I longed to be part of their world, I realized that they were trying to shield me from the darkness that could easily pull me in. It was a bittersweet feeling—wanting to connect with my brothers while recognizing the dangers that came with it.

Then, my sister Leisa ended up moving into the same projects where our grandmother and mother once lived. It was like the cycle had come full circle. By the late 1990s and early 2000s, however, the Ripley Arnold Projects began to be viewed differently. People saw them as a symbol of the struggles associated with public housing. Concerns about safety and crime grew, leading to plans to tear down the old buildings and replace them with new ones.

After the closing of Glen Garden, we found new apartments called The Ambassadors. They were small, but we ended up right back in Blood territory off Lancaster Avenue. Fortunately, there wasn't much gang activity inside our building, but the apartments next door and behind us had a lot of Bloods living there.

Kevin and Kasey used to hang out together a lot and would frequently walk all the way from The Ambassadors to downtown where the projects were located, which was a five-mile walk. I admired their determination, but I also worried about them walking through those neighborhoods. They seemed unfazed by the risks, though, treating each walk as an adventure.

Years before the projects were closed for good, Kevin, Kasey, and several of their friends contributed to the issues that led to the demolition. Their actions added to the challenges that the community faced, making it difficult for the projects to thrive. The story of the Ripley Arnold Projects is a mix of family history, struggles, and the desire for a better life, showing how the past can echo through generations.

Kevin had been getting into trouble, selling fake crack, hustling for money, just living that street life. I remember him being so proud of himself, flashing all that money, acting like he was somebody. But deep down, I knew it was all smoke and mirrors. He didn't know it back then, but he was heading down a path that would take him far from me.

One day, Kevin, Kasey, and a few friends found themselves in the projects when they ran right into a group of police officers.

When Kevin and Kasey spotted the cops, they quickly started walking in the other direction. The officers called out for them to stop, but they kept moving, hearts racing. Kevin then asked everyone, "Are y'all dirty?" This was their way of checking if anyone had drugs on them. Everyone said no, so they thought they were safe.

As they turned a corner, Kasey suddenly took off running into the street. Kevin yelled after him, telling him to stop and said, "You said you're not dirty, right?" But by then, the police were right behind them, asking for IDs and questioning where they were going and if they lived in the projects; they were only thirteen and fourteen.

While the officers questioned them, they began shining their flashlights around. Suddenly, one of the officers found a baggie of crack on the ground and held it up. Then, one of the cops walked up to Kevin and said, "It was him; I saw him throw it." They were lying, but the police didn't want to hear his side. They put him in the back of a police car, and Kasey, upset, started asking why they were taking his brother away. To his surprise, they put Kasey in the car with him.

They were taken to juvenile detention, which they called "Kimbo Road," located at 2701 Kimbo Rd. While sitting in the car, Kasey offered to tell the police that the crack was his, but Kevin told him not to worry; he had it handled.

He had been to juvenile detention several times before, but this time felt different. The judge found him guilty and sentenced him to the Texas Youth

Commission (TYC). Kasey often said this was when everything started to go downhill for our family. Kevin, the oldest, had been trying to take the blame for Kasey, believing it would help him out. Instead, he ended up in a place that would change his life forever.

While at TYC, he saw many other kids who were also struggling with their own problems. Some had made mistakes similar to his, while others were dealing with deeper issues. It was a tough place, but he began to realize that he could either let it break him or use it to grow. He wanted to make a change for himself and for our family.

A few nights before Kevin made his choice and was sent the juvenile, I remember he and I were riding together in a truck he had stolen. We headed downtown so he could confront this old-school guy named Walter, who had been owing him money for a while. When we pulled into these efficiency apartments, we thought we saw him. But when we knocked on the door, no one answered. We went back upstairs to his apartment, certain he was ducking us. When we knocked on the door again and yelled, "I know you're in there!" Kevin kicked the door in.

We went inside and started searching the room for anything of value, and that's when we found Walter hiding behind the couch. Kevin asked him, "Why are you hiding? Where's my money?" He tried to lie, and in that moment, Kevin knocked him out. The guy literally started snoring right there on the floor. I remember Kevin saying, "Watch this," and leaning back to hit him. As soon as he hit him, I said, "Man, you better not ever hit me again." He promised he wouldn't, and he kept that promise. It was a wild day, but it was one of those moments that stuck with me.

I thought about the day he went to juvenile detention and how it broke something in me. A part of me wanted to follow him, to be where he was, to figure out what it was like inside, even though I knew I wasn't ready for that life. But deep down, I realized something: we were both trapped. Trapped in different ways. Kevin, in the system, and me, in a world that didn't seem to care about people like us.

Kevin had always been the wild one. He was like me in many ways, but more reckless. He had this fire inside him, and he wasn't afraid to let it burn. Growing up on the Southside of Fort Worth, we lived through the same struggles: drugs, violence, and the lack of any real structure in our lives. But Kevin? He seemed determined to make his own way in the world, even if it meant making the wrong choices.

I didn't understand the full weight of what Kevin was going through at the time. Sure, we were in the same world, but I was managing to stay under the radar.

As time went on, I began noticing the cracks in his armor. At first, it was the way he started hanging with the wrong crowd. The guys who weren't just about selling drugs, but were about taking lives. Kevin wasn't a killer—not yet. But he was surrounded by those who were, and that kind of energy was contagious.

It wasn't long after that is when things escalated. A fight broke out at OD Wyatt, the high school I was attending before I dropped out after Glen Garden closed. It started over something stupid—someone wearing the wrong color. But, as always, the little things turned into something much bigger. Those guys didn't think twice; they didn't consider that I had to go to this school once they left. Fists flew, bottles shattered, and even a crutch was used. Soon, it was more than just a fight; it became a war for respect.

Kevin was right in the middle of it, and he wasn't backing down. I remember seeing him at the center of the chaos, shouting something at a guy from the other side. His face was twisted in rage, and for the first time, I realized how far Kevin had fallen into this world.

"Kevin!" I yelled, trying to reach him through the noise. But he didn't hear me. He didn't care. He was already beyond me, beyond us. In that moment, I felt a mix of fear and sadness, knowing that the brother I looked up to was getting lost in this madness. I could only watch as the fight raged on, feeling helpless as the world around us spiraled into chaos.

That was the first time I felt that wall between us. A wall that had always been there but was now so much thicker. I realized then that the streets had him—they had all of us, really—but Kevin had bought in more than most. His pride was tied to the hood, to the flag, and to the power he had. He had become something I couldn't recognize. And as much as I wanted to keep him from going down the wrong path, I knew deep down that I couldn't save him.

It wasn't just about survival anymore. It was about reputation, and that meant everything to him. It was a strange kind of loyalty we had, even among the madness. We were all a part of the same mess. And Kevin? He'd gotten tangled in it deeper than any of us realized. The drug game, the violence, the constant threat of death—it became his reality. And that's when the streets, and all the chaos that came with it, started to consume him.

But here's where things took a turn for the worse: after that first arrest, Kevin didn't back down. He got caught again, and again, and the cycle just kept repeating itself. The system was built to break people like Kevin. And it almost did.

There were times, when we were kids, that Kevin would talk about getting out. He had dreams—dumb ones, maybe, but dreams, nonetheless. He said he wanted to get his hands on enough cash to leave the block behind, to get away from all the violence and drugs. He wanted to disappear. And for a while, I believed him. I thought, maybe, just maybe, he could be different. But as he got older, I saw that spark start to fade. The more he got caught up in the system, the more he turned into someone I didn't recognize.

When he got arrested that last time, I could feel it in my bones—he wasn't coming out the same. The juvenile detention center? It was a stepping stone. But the juvenile prison system, TYC? That would break him.

I tried visiting him, tried keeping in touch, but each time, it was harder. His letters became shorter, his words colder. The system didn't just punish you for your crimes—it punished you for dreaming, for trying to be something different. And slowly, Kevin stopped trying.

By the time he was transferred to TYC, I knew it was too late. There was no way out for him—not unless he fought with everything he had. And by then, the fight had left him.

That's when I realized that the real fight wasn't out here, on the streets, with rival sets or the police. It was a fight inside. And Kevin had already lost that battle.

Kevin going to jail was really hard for me because he was my protector, like a dad to me. Since our uncle had been locked up, he had taken on the role of the man of the house, always looking out for us. When he went to TYC, I was devastated and felt a huge sense of loss. But at least I still had my other big brother Kasey and my little brother Brandon with me, at least for now. I knew I had to lean on them and stay strong, but it was tough not having Kevin by my side.

Chapter Fifteen

The Price of Loyalty

"Loyalty is not about who you stand with, but about who you choose to stand for."

You ever look back and wonder how you got here? How you ended up in this mess, with no clear way out? I think about it all the time, especially when it comes to Brandon. My little brother. The one who was always kinda lost in the shuffle. You see, Brandon wasn't like the rest of us. I mean, we all had our issues, but him? He carried something different, something deeper.

I remember our childhood on Stewart Street, playing football in the street. Brandon was different from the rest of us. He ran around without shoes and, for some strange reason, he didn't wear underwear. It wasn't because he didn't want to; it was mostly because he wet the bed so much that our family couldn't buy him any.

Brandon in State School

Brandon was quiet and always seemed to be watching from the sidelines. He didn't quite fit in, and nobody really asked what he was thinking. But I could see something in his eyes—a lot was going on beneath the surface.

There was a darkness inside him, something similar to what I had seen in Kevin, but it felt even deeper. I don't think anyone ever tried to understand it, or maybe they were just too scared to.

Looking back, I wonder how many times we missed the chance to reach out to someone who seemed different. How many stories were left untold because we didn't ask the right questions?

You see, Kevin, Kasey, and even me, we had our own fights. We could get rough with each other, but it wasn't the same with Brandon. We'd beat up on him, push him around, but there was something in us that knew we were making him stronger. It was like we were all carrying our own baggage, but his was heavier than ours. He couldn't catch a break from anybody. Not from me, not from Kasey, and sure as heck not from Kevin.

When we were younger, I tried to figure out how to deal with him. Kevin and Kasey got along, but I couldn't connect with Brandon. I remember when Grama started letting me get at him — "whoop him", she said. Maybe she thought I could do it better than her. But I was wrong. I wasn't the right one to teach him; I wasn't even the right one to teach myself. I thought I was helping, later I found out that all I was doing was making him angrier. And what was worse, he started taking that anger out on people around him. That's when he started acting out. He wasn't afraid to fight — he'd fight anybody if it meant he could get the attention he craved.

But no one really saw him. I saw him. I saw the cracks in him, the places where he was broken. He wasn't just angry at us; he was angry at everything, at the world, at life. And honestly? I didn't blame him.

Brandon's story is complicated, and you'll find out more about it later; it's all mixed up with the choices he made. But it goes deeper than that. He didn't know how to make the right choices because he didn't have anyone to guide him. While Kevin and I didn't have a close relationship with our fathers, we at least had some idea of who they were. Brandon, on the other hand, wasn't sure about his dad. He only knew that JB might be his father, or maybe it was Duke, who looked at him and said, "That ain't mine."

One of the biggest problems with not having a father or any male role model is the emotional and mental impact it has on a young man. Without someone to look up to, Brandon struggled, just like we all did, with learning social skills and figuring out what it means to be a man. When Uncle Michael went to jail, Brandon was left with us as his older brothers to guide him and be as role models. I had a lot of support from Kevin and Kasey, they never really wanted me to get into any trouble, but Brandon—he didn't have that same guidance. He felt alone in this world, and it showed in everything he did. His anger, confusion, and constant fights were all cries for help. I just didn't know how to give him what he needed.

At home, it was usually just me, Brandon, and Leisa left to fend for ourselves. Many mornings, we woke up with our stomachs growling from hunger. There was no food in the house, and no adults around to help us, so we had to find a way to survive.

We would grab the big coats Uncle Lawrence had left behind while he was in jail—coats that still held his smell, a mix of cigarettes and something else we couldn't quite place. We huddled into them, hoping they would hide our skinny bodies as we headed to the grocery store called Max, right across from our apartments on Lancaster Avenue.

As we walked, our hearts raced with a mix of excitement and fear. We knew stealing food was wrong, but the hunger pushed us to go anyway. Inside Max, we felt a strange mix of freedom and guilt. Leisa and Brandon were quick at finding what we needed.

They would dart through the aisles, grabbing bologna, cheese, bread, and cereal, shoving them into the big coats we wore like bags.

We kept an eye out for store workers or security, our hearts pounding every time someone walked in. It was a risky game, but we felt we had no choice. The thought of going back home empty-handed felt unbearable. We had to keep each other motivated, whispering encouragement as we quietly stuffed food into our coats, hoping we wouldn't get caught.

After gathering what we could, we'd sneak out of the store, feeling a mix of guilt and relief. Once we were outside, we rushed back home, ready to share our stolen food. Sitting together on the old couch, we'd unwrap our stash, feeling like we had accomplished something important. In those moments, we weren't just surviving; we were sticking together against the world, finding a way to make it through another day.

After Kevin went to TYC, Kasey felt he needed to step up and take on the big brother role, especially since he felt responsible for Kevin going to jail. Kasey started working with his dad doing yard work, but then one day that stopped.

Kasey's relationship with our grandmother was tense; she really didn't like him. So, while other boys his age were at home with their families at night, Kasey had to fend for himself. Sure, he had a dad, but their relationship was rocky. And our mom, well, drugs—specifically crack—had her so caught up that she often didn't have a place to live. Most of the time, she lived with Grama, who wouldn't let Kasey inside the house.

Kasey became known as "Lil AGG," and with that name came a reputation. Many of us younger kids looked up to him, and Brandon was one of his biggest fans. He did everything Kasey told him to do.

And that's when I started seeing things for what they were. I was mad. I was angry. But we had to make a choice. I learned that the hard way. And Brandon? He learned it too, but it was like he didn't know how. He had the same choices, but it felt like he didn't have the strength to make the right ones. He kept falling into the same patterns. I could see it. I could feel it in my bones.

One night, Kasey gave a gun to a kid named Chris, who was good friends with Brandon, and told us how to rob someone. I was fourteen, and Chris and Brandon were twelve. We made our way across the street to the Max grocery store, where cars were parked and customers were loading their groceries. We started to check out the scene.

Then we spotted her—a woman alone in her car who seemed like an easy target. Part of me was really scared, but I wanted to be cool. I wanted Brandon to respect me like he respected Kasey, so I went along with it. As we approached her vehicle, the lady, who was White, must have seen us in her mirror because as soon as we got close, she hurriedly locked the doors.

Some people might have been offended by that, but I didn't blame her. If I saw three young black boys wearing baggy clothes and hats walking up to my car, I would have been nervous too. The moment she locked her doors, Brandon grabbed the handle, but she started to drive away. I thought, well, that's that, and I felt relieved.

But then Chris pulled out the gun that Kasey had given him—a black Glock .380. He pulled back the handle to put a bullet in the chamber and aimed it at the lady's car. I was in shock as he pulled the trigger. We ran away fast. Everyone laughed and high-fived Chris, treating him like a hero for what he had just done.

But I was terrified. The lady was safe and unharmed, but all I could think about was what could have happened. What if he had shot her? What if he had killed her?

If Chris had shot the lady, those of us who were with him—like Brandon and me—could have faced charges too, even if we didn't directly participate in the act. This is known as "accessory liability." If you're present during a crime and you encourage or assist the person committing the crime in any way, you might be charged as an accessory or accomplice. This means you could be held responsible for the crime, even if you didn't physically do anything illegal yourself.

Thinking about all of this made me realize how much danger we were in just by being there that night. It wasn't just Chris who could have faced the consequences; we all could have had our lives changed forever because of one reckless decision.

That night, as I ran away from the scene, I realized that I didn't want to be involved in something that could lead to such terrible consequences. The weight of that possibility hung heavy in my mind, making me realize that I needed to distance myself from Kasey and the risky choices he was making.

I tried to encourage Brandon to start hanging out with me instead of getting into trouble. I was dating a girl who had a sister that really liked Brandon. I thought it would be fun for us to hang out with them instead of running around trying to rob people. But Brandon wasn't interested in my idea. He looked at me the way so many others did, like I was different for not wanting to do dangerous things. I was considered a square. But in the end, I hoped that my choice would pay off.

Weeks after the incident in the Max parking lot, Brandon was at it again. This time, he chose a man who was walking from the store as his target. Brandon approached him with the same .380 gun and said, "Give me all your money." The man replied, "All I have is 67 cents," and Brandon took it. Brandon was young and naïve and didn't realize that what he just did was armed robbery. What was even more disturbing was that this happened right across the street from where we lived.

Days after the incident, the man spotted Brandon and followed him home. As Brandon entered our apartment, the man called the police. The next day, the police showed up at our door. My grandmother answered, and the police asked if a young man lived there. Since she had already told Brandon that he was no longer welcome at her home, she figured they were talking about me. This was one of the rare times I found myself at school, which is what my grandmother told the police.

The officers went to Polytechnic High School, where I was attending, and called me to the office. Luckily, they couldn't identify me and went back to our house to ask my grandmother if they could search the apartment. She agreed. To our surprise, my sister Leisa had let Brandon inside without my grandmother knowing and had hidden him in the closet. The police pulled him out, and the man he robbed identified him. Brandon was just twelve years old and now facing charges for armed robbery.

He was taken to Kimbo Road and thought he would get out like he had in the past. But this time was different.

Ambassadors had a reputation for crime, and during our time there, the city was threatening to shut it down. A murder had recently occurred, and Brandon's name came up in the investigation. During his interrogation, the detectives told him he was not only facing armed robbery but also a murder charge. Brandon began to tell them what he knew about the murder, which involved our brother Kasey. This would create tension between the two of them for years.

Ultimately, Brandon was sentenced to TYC and sent to Gainesville, Texas. I felt horrible. How could I let this happen to my little brother? Now the only brother I had left was Kasey, and he was facing charges for murder.

Chapter Sixteen

When the Walls Close In

"When the world you know crumbles beneath your feet, you learn just how far you're willing to fall."

I remember that day like it was yesterday — the day my brother Kasey got arrested. I was fourteen years old, just a kid who didn't fully understand what was happening, but I knew it was bad. And I knew my brother was about to be locked away for a long time.

Kasey had always been the tough one. The one who everyone looked up to, who seemed like he could take on the world. But that day, when I saw the police car pull up outside The Ambassador Apartments, something in me cracked. It was real now. He wasn't untouchable. And I couldn't stop it.

I had already heard the rumors. The detectives had been following Kasey for a while. They were looking for him. They said he had a date to turn himself in, or they'd come knocking on his door. I didn't want to believe it, but there were too many signs. When I saw the detectives sitting in their cars outside, watching, waiting for him to slip up, I felt it in my gut.

I ran to Kasey. "Yo, they're looking for you, man. They've been talking about you on the streets, saying you need to turn yourself in, or it's gonna get worse," I told him, out of breath. He didn't seem worried though. Kasey always had this cocky swagger, like he was too slick to get caught.

The mood in the house was tense as I heard heavy footsteps coming toward the door. Suddenly, there was a loud knock, and my heart started pounding. When I opened the door, I was shocked to see a group of task force police officers standing there, their serious faces mostly hidden by the typical masks they wear.

The masks added an extra layer of intensity to the moment, making it hard to read their expressions.

The officers were dressed in uniforms and vests, with their badges clearly visible and weapons drawn. They moved with confidence, commanding authority as one shouted, "Everybody get on the floor!"

But my grandmother didn't budge. "I'm not getting on no floor," she replied defiantly, her voice steady despite the chaos.

Officer Ferguson stepped forward, his tone firm but calm. "We're looking for Kasey," he said, trying to reassure her.

I felt a mix of fear and confusion. The officers stepped inside, their presence filling our small apartment. They spread out, searching each room carefully, speaking quietly but authoritatively to each other. I could see the determination in their eyes; they were on a mission.

Questions raced through my mind. Where was my brother? What are they going to do to him? As the officers searched, I laid on the floor frozen, trying to understand what was happening. I could hear them calling out for my brother, their voices echoing through the quiet rooms.

Every moment felt stretched with anxiety and uncertainty. I looked around, noticing how everything seemed different with the police here—in our home, usually a place of comfort, now felt like a scene from a dramatic movie.

As the search went on, I realized how serious the situation was, not just for me, but for my brother, who was out there somewhere. I hoped he was safe, even as the officers moved through our space with determination, looking for answers that could change everything for our family.

Suddenly, I heard a crackle from one of the officers' walkie-talkies. "We got him," came the voice, clear and final. My heart sank, and a rush of emotions hit me all at once—fear, confusion, and a deep sense of helplessness.

Without thinking, I jumped up and ran outside, my feet pounding against the ground as panic fueled my movements. I burst through the door, the cool air hitting my face like a splash of cold water. My heart raced as I scanned the area, searching for my brother.

Then, I saw him. He was standing there, handcuffed, surrounded by a couple of officers. A mixture of shock and sadness flooded over me. His face looked tense, and the reality of the situation hit me hard. Seeing him in those cuffs made my stomach twist. I wanted to rush to him, to ask what had happened, to tell him that everything would be okay, but fear held me back.

My brother looked lost and vulnerable, and it broke my heart to see him like that. The anger I felt toward the situation, toward the officers, and even toward my brother for getting caught all swirled together. I wanted to scream, to fight against this injustice, but all I could do was stand there, feeling small and powerless.

I couldn't stop what was happening. I saw my mom standing there, looking at Kasey like he had just betrayed her, but I could tell she was broken too. I saw my grandmother's face too—cold, distant. She'd always known something was coming. Always had that "I told you so" look.

I remember Kasey asking Officer Ferguson if he could hug momma before they took him in. Ferguson gave him a nod. It was like a small gesture, but that moment… it felt like a lifetime. I never thought I'd see Kasey hug her for the last time. He was a man now, and there was no going back.

My brother wasn't just another hoodlum off the streets. He was family. My blood. And watching him disappear like that, knowing I couldn't save him... It messed me up.

But it wasn't just the arrest that stung. It was everything that led up to it. Kasey, always the protector, but that was the price of his choices.

Kasey in age 15 Sentenced as an adult

Kasey was fifteen, just a kid himself, but it felt like he was already a man hardened by years of struggle.

And when I went to see him a few days later, it hit me. This wasn't the same Kasey I'd known. The walls were closing in on him. He looked different—hollow in a way. His eyes were still sharp, but there was a darkness I hadn't seen before. His fight had always been physical, but now it was mental.

The worst part? Kasey didn't even have time to process what had happened. No time to breathe or heal. The weight of it all—the arrest, the streets, the violence, the anger—it all crashed into him at once.

But the hardest part? When Kasey found out that momma had been the one to turn him in for the reward money. Her son, her flesh and blood, the one person he would've died for… she had betrayed him. And that was a wound that couldn't heal, not for a long time.

There was no trial, just a confession. "I did it," he said, and those words hung heavily in the air. When he stood before the judge, tried as an adult as a teenager, the weight of the moment hit me like a punch to the gut. Twenty years was the sentence, and in those cold courtroom walls, his life was determined with a gavel's strike. I felt utterly powerless, unable to do anything to stop it.

The Kasey I knew was gone. The boy I looked up to, the one who used to protect me and make me feel safe, was now the one in chains. My heart ached as I thought about him stand there, his head bowed, the light in his eyes dimmed by the harsh reality of his situation.

Memories flooded my mind—his laughter, the way he would always stand up for me against anyone who tried to harm me. Now, that same boy was being led away, his future stolen in an instant. I felt a mix of anger and sorrow, not just for him but for all the dreams that had vanished in that courtroom.

The world outside continued as if nothing had changed, but for me, everything was different. The bond we had was shattered, and in that moment, I realized that the man I once admired was trapped in a nightmare, and I could do nothing to pull him back.

Now, Uncle Michael, Uncle Lawrence, Kevin, Kasey, and Brandon were all in jail, leaving a gaping hole in our family. The weight of their absence felt like a heavy blanket. With Grama sick and in the hospital, everything seemed to spiral further out of control. Momma, overwhelmed by it all, decided to send Leisa to stay with her dad's family. That left just me and Momma, and the thought filled me with dread.

In her usual chaotic way, Momma went on a smoking spree. Before she slipped out, she handed me the food stamp card, her eyes hazy and unfocused. "Make sure you keep this safe," she said, her voice a mix of urgency and desperation. I knew it was to prevent her from spending it all on crack. I nodded, feeling the weight of responsibility sit on my shoulders, even at just fourteen.

As I waited, I could sense the storm brewing inside her. When she returned, I recognized the signs immediately—her spaced-out look and the way she chewed spearmint gum, a habit that always made me cringe. I hated the sight of it; it reminded me of the chaos that consumed her.

"Momma, we need those stamps," I said, my voice trembling. "It's just us now, and Grama can't help us if we go broke."

Her reaction was swift and explosive. She screamed and yelled, and I felt my heart race with fear and frustration. Unable to stay in the suffocating atmosphere a moment longer, I stormed out, needing to escape.

When I returned, my heart sank at the sight before me. Momma had taken all the food from the refrigerator and thrown it onto the floor, into the trash, and even in the sink. There she stood, pouring milk onto the floor as if it were a statement of defiance. "If I can't have the food stamps, then you can't have the food!" she shouted, and my anger boiled over.

"Get out!" I yelled, grabbing her arm in a moment of desperation. I knew I was risking her wrath. She was strong when high, and as she pushed past me and left the apartment, I felt a mix of relief and fear.

Then, from outside, I heard a loud crash that sent chills down my spine. I rushed to the window just in time to see her throw a brick through the glass of my room. "No way!" I gasped, horror-stricken. Soon after, she called the police, claiming she was going to kill herself. They arrived quickly, and the sight of the flashing lights outside our apartment was surreal. The officers informed me that I couldn't stay alone, given my age.

Embarrassment washed over me as I looked out at the neighbors who gathered outside, whispers spreading like wildfire. With no one else to turn to, I thought of Aunt Cat, Carolyn Norwood, the mother of

Uncle Michael's youngest child. I had known her all my life, and she had come through for me in the past.

When Aunt Cat pulled up, her car was a beacon of hope in the chaos. "Where is my nephew?" she asked, concern fixed on her face. I felt a rush of gratitude as I explained I was temporarily staying with a neighbor. Her presence brought a sense of comfort, and I respected her for stepping in when I needed it most.

Meanwhile, the reality of my family's situation weighed heavily on my mind. Kevin was in TYC, Kasey was in county jail waiting to be tried as an adult, and Brandon was in juvenile detention, awaiting sentencing. My sister was with her dad's family, Momma was in the mental ward, and Grama was sick in the hospital. It felt like everything had fallen apart, and I was left to pick up the pieces.

Aunt Cat offered me a place to stay, but deep down, I wanted to go home. I returned to our apartment, determined to clean up the mess and speak with the landlord about fixing the broken windows. Despite being only fourteen, I was determined to handle things on my own.

I didn't go wild or throw parties. I had one good friend, Derrick Brown, and we would hang out, but I knew better than to let anyone disturb the fragile peace of my grandmother's home. I remember trying to cook chicken for the first time, wanting to recreate the meals Grama used to make. I soaked the chicken in the sink, mixed salt and pepper with the flour, and heated the Crisco in the skillet, just like she taught me.

But when I sat down to eat, the sight of the raw chicken shocked me. I poured ketchup onto my plate, lifted my fork, and saw the blood run from the meat. I dropped my fork in horror and cried, the frustration of my life crashing down around me.

The next day, I rode the bus to the hospital to visit my grandmother at Osteopathic Hospital, located on Camp Bowie Drive, directly across from the University of North Texas Health Science Center. As I stepped off the bus, I saw students bustling around, unaware of the struggles I was facing. Their ambition inspired me, and I hoped to find some strength for myself.

Every day, I sat by her side as she grew sicker. I didn't understand the medical jargon at the time—she was septic and suffering from a form of encephalopathy—but I understood the fear of losing her. I remember one day, as a storm raged outside, they had to move all the patients into the hall for safety. Grama looked up at me, her eyes searching. "You still here? Why aren't you at school?" she asked, and I realized how much I needed to be there for her.

After we moved from Glen Garden to Ambassadors, I decided it was time to return to school. I transferred to Poly Tech, away from the chaos of OD Wyatt, but without supervision or motivation, I only sporadically attended.

Then came that fateful Friday. After school, I returned to the hospital. As I walked through the automatic sliding doors, I felt a sense of dread wash over me. I was about to step onto the elevator when I spotted my mother sitting in the waiting area. She got up and rushed toward me, tears streaming down her face. She wasn't there to apologize but was trying to say something important. Before she could get it out, they wheeled my grandmother past us on a stretcher after amputating her leg. The sight shattered me, and I broke down in tears.

When I was finally allowed into her room, Grama looked at me with a glimmer of lucidity. "Are you mad at me?" she asked softly, and I shook my head, wrapping my arms around her. "No, I'm mad at myself. I should not have left you." From that moment on, I vowed to stay by her side.

Once again, I returned home to an empty apartment, listening to the rain pounding against the windows, feeling a sense of fear—not of the storm, but of losing my grandmother. It was March 1995, and I had never truly prayed before. Yes, my mother had taught us how, but I didn't understand its power until that moment of desperation.

I dropped to my knees, tears streaming down my face, crying out to God, "Please don't take her." In that moment, I promised that if He let her live, I would do better, get back in school, and prepare for whatever came next. I needed a miracle. I needed her.

Letter From Me to You!

As I sit here, reflecting on everything that's happened, I can't help but feel like the real story hasn't even started yet. The four of us—me, Kevin, Brandon, and Kasey—are all fighting different battles, each of us drowning in a sea of secrets and lies, trying to survive this nightmare called life. But the walls of this place, they're closing in, and I can feel the pressure building. There's so much more you don't know yet. So many things I haven't told you—things that, when they finally come to light, could change everything.

As I looked over statistics, I couldn't help but wonder: Am I destined to fail? The phrase "No Child Left Behind" echoes in my mind, a hollow promise from the Bush era that reminds me of my own struggles growing up. A child should not be born into a situation where they have to fight every day just to survive. Yet, this is the reality for many, and it was mine as well.

Every day, I faced the harsh truths of life, battling against the odds stacked high against me. I learned that I was part of the "Fatherless Generation," with a staggering 71% chance of dropping out of high school—nine times the average rate. Those numbers felt like chains binding me, whispering that I never had a chance. I grew up in a drug-infested home, a place where emotional and psychological stress was the norm, where worries about what was happening at home soaked into every aspect of my life, including school.

The idea of finishing high school seemed like a distant dream, let alone attending college. I often thought about the lack of support in my home, where no one had the education to help me with Algebra or Chemistry. The weight of those statistics pressed down on me, filling my heart with doubt and fear.

But here's the truth I've discovered along the way: "Excuses are tools used by incompetent individuals that build monuments that lead to nothingness." I realized that while statistics may depict a grim future, they do not dictate it. I refused to be defined by my circumstances. I chose to fight against the narrative that said I was destined to fail.

As I listened to the lyrics of "Dream" by William Murphy — "It's never too late to be what you should've been; It's never too late to start over again; It's never too late to do what you should've done; The curses are gone, you are the chosen one" — these words continue to echo in my head today. They serve as a powerful reminder that no matter where we come from, our potential remains intact, waiting to be unleashed.

So, I have come to the conclusion that everyone has a story, but it is what you do with your story that counts. To anyone who feels trapped by their situation, know this: Your past does not define your future. Yes, life can be incredibly difficult, and the odds may seem impossible, but God can give you the power to change your story. It won't be easy, and there will be challenges at every turn, but perseverance, determination, and faith in something bigger than your situation, can pave the way for a brighter tomorrow.

Remember, you are not alone. Many have walked the path you are on, and many have risen above it. Use your struggles as fuel to propel you forward, and let your dreams guide you. It's time to break the cycle, to rewrite your narrative, and to rise above the statistics.

With all the chaos you have read, there's more to come. What happened to Grama? What happened to Momma? Did Leisa just fall off the face of the earth? How did Kevin and Brandon survive in state school? Did Kasey manage to survive in jail as a teenager?

Hold tight, because this is only the beginning. What's coming next—well, let's just say it's going to be a whole lot harder to stay in the dark. The truth is more tangled than I ever imagined, and the stakes are higher than ever.

As the shadows close in, I'm ready to uncover the secrets that bind us. The journey ahead promises to be filled with challenges, revelations, and unexpected twists. So, if you think you've seen it all, just wait. The real story is only just unfolding. —*TGBTG!!!*

Made in the USA
Columbia, SC
17 June 2025